THE
NYMPHOMANIAC

*A Study in the Origins of
a Passion of the Soul*

A Psycho-Mythology Series

A SMALL GEM

Copyright © 1985 J. Marvin Spiegelman

All rights reserved. No part of this book,
in part or in whole, may be reproduced, transmitted,
or utilized, in any form or by any means, electronic or mechanical,
including photocopying, recording, or by any information storage
and retrieval system, without permission in writing
from the publisher, except for brief quotations
in critical articles, books and reviews.

ISBN 13: 978-1-56184-504-0
ISBN 10: 1-56184-504-3

First Edition 1985

New Falcon Publications Second Revised Edition 2022

The paper used in this publication meets the minimum requirements
of the American National Standard for Permanence of
Paper for Printed Library Materials Z39.48-1984

Printed in USA

NEW FALCON PUBLICATIONS

2046 Hillhurst Avenue
Los Angeles, CA 90027
www.newfalcon.com
email: info@newfalcon.com

THE
NYMPHOMANIAC

*A Study in the Origins of
a Passion of the Soul*

A Psycho-Mythology Series

A SMALL GEM

J. MARVIN SPIEGELMAN, Ph.D.

NEW FALCON PUBLICATIONS
Los Angeles, California, U.S.A.

Other Titles by J. Marvin Spiegelman, Ph.D.

A Modern Jew in Search of Soul

Buddhism and Jungian Psychology

Catholicism and Jungian Psychology

Hinduism and Jungian Psychology

Mysticism, Psychology and Oedipus - A Small Gem

Protestanism and Jungian Psychology

Psychotherapy and Religion at the Millennium and Beyond

Psychotherapy as a Mutual Process

Reich, Jung, Regardie & Me - The Unhealed Healer

Rider, Haggard, Henry Miller & I - The Unpublished Writer

Sufism, Islam and Jungian Psychology

The Knight - A Small Gem

The Nymphomaniac

The Quest - Further Adventures in the Unconscious

The Tree of Life - Paths in Jungian Individuation

The Wisdom of J. Marvin Speigelman
  Volume I - Selected Writings

The Wisdom of J. Marvin Speigelman
  Volume II - Psychology and Religion

MANY OF OUR TITLES AVAILABLE ON KINDLE!
Please visit our website at http://www.newfalcon.com

CONTENTS

CHAPTER 1
Sybilla, The Nymphomaniac   1

CHAPTER 2
Developmental Possibilities in
Active Imagination   47

CHAPTER 3
The Potentials and Limitations of
Active Imagination   51

CHAPTER 4
Commentary on the Nymphomaniac   81

CHAPTER 1
SYBILLA,
THE NYMPHOMANIAC

My name is Sybilla. Julia, like you, I want to tell my name; I also like to know names. In my feeling, this desire is not just a feminine or individual trait, as you seem to think, Julia. My need arises from pain. I have had more than enough of experiencing men and Gods with no names. The nameless, the impersonal, has occupied a large part of my life. It has brought me hurt, pain–no, how can I even use these pale words? The impersonal and the nameless have brought me agony. That will be apparent from my story.

I am glad to be here, and I belong among you. I know that, though at one time I did not believe that I belonged anywhere! That, too, will be understood from my tale. Where shall I begin? I suppose I should explain why I should be called "The Nymphomaniac." I would prefer that my story unfold as it is, and, in due time, you will understand how it was I have had that title. Ah, titles, that brings me to the beginning of my story.

I was born in Alexandria of an Egyptian Crown Prince. That is what I was told by my mother. I tell you that is what my mother told me, and I tell you in such a way as to make you doubt whether I believe it. Well, in point of fact, I do not believe it. I believe my mother's story all right, but I am not convinced that I am her daughter, let alone the daughter of an Egyptian Crown Prince. Before I explain that, let me tell the story as my mother told me. It is a little sad, a little sordid, and a little beautiful. All three. At least I think it is all three.

My mother, may her soul not suffer again, was a pretty little Greek girl, on holiday from the country. She happened to meet a handsome young sailor one day, who was also on holiday from his ship. The young sailor, in point of fact, was the Crown Prince

of Egypt, learning to sail ships, as young royalty do. He was on shore leave and wandering about in the Greek capitol city when he espied my mother, with her golden blond hair, brown eyes, and marvelous figure. The Prince was dark and handsome and Arab. They looked at each other and fell in love. At first, the Prince would not tell my mother who he was–he wanted to be loved for himself, of course. My mother was so loving and loyal, obviously devoted and genuine, however, that he had to be honest with her, and told her the good news. You may detect a note of irony as I tell the story. I have seen so much of life that such pleasant little fairy tales make me sound a little wry. I am sorry to be bitter about it–I had thought that all bitterness and regret and irony had vanished from my soul, but apparently not. Perhaps, the mere telling of my tale will dispel the last remnants of bitterness that reside therein. So, let me go on with my mother's story. In truth, I am more sorry for her pain than for my own.

The couple fell in love, as I have said, and swore undying devotion to each other. He got away from his ship, and she from her family, both with lies and excuses which were readily believed since they had been so truthful and ingenuous before. They traveled to the great holy places of Greece on a kind of pre-marital honeymoon. The sights were an all new adventure for my father, of course, but so was it for my mother, who had lived the life of a happy pleasant girl.

The couple was much in love, my mother tells me. They spent their first night in Delphi, where, she says, I was conceived. My mother told me that night was one of ecstasy for them both–they felt that they were totally united with each other, that their love was destined by God, both his Moslem and her Greek Orthodox Christian God. That may well be, but I think differently. My view may have sounded strange to you before, when I said that I do not believe I am my mother's daughter. Now I can explain. I do not think that it was the Moslem God nor the Orthodox Christian God that sanctioned and brought together their love the night I was conceived. No. I believe that the Ancient Greek Gods and the Ancient Egyptian Gods were let loose that marvelous-terrible night, and I was born as a consequence. A blessing, you might say? Wait until you hear my story and see if you still think so.

My mother and father fulfilled their love near the Omphallos, the Navel of the World, the Center of the Universe, on the hard ground, late at night, under the stars, believing that they were having a great lark. Well, may the Gods forgive them, they were young and carefree and unknowing. They–at least my mother, I am not sure about my father–suffered enough for that night, I think, and I have suffered for it, too, but, they, at least, had their pleasure and joy.

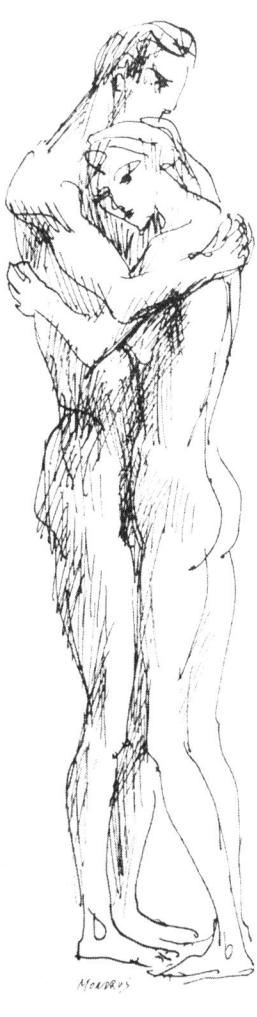

After a few days, my father returned to his ship and my mother to her farm, he promising to write to her soon, as soon as he could get his father's consent for marriage. My mother was radiant and joyous. When she returned to her family on the farm, she told her parents and family the story in the naive belief that they would be happy, too. Naturally, they were shocked and skeptical. They simply beat her. Such were some peasants in those days, and, I suppose, such are some peasants at every period of history–and not only peasants, as I can tell you from my experience, but city folk, too.

My mother wept from this pain and disappointment in her family, but she took heart in the hope that her prince, who was, of course, *the Prince*, would take her to a new life.

Time went by and there was no word from the prince. My mother missed one menstrual period, and then another, and it was clear that she was pregnant from that fateful night. At last, a letter came from my father. In it he announced, tearfully, that his father would not give his consent to the marriage of a future king to a common peasant girl, even if the girl were the finest in the world. It was not a matter of cruelty or love, the young prince could have all the love affairs that he wished. No, the prince was betrothed, without his knowledge, to a proper young princess of a different country, and this arrangement was good for both countries; their personal feelings and desires had no bearing in any of it.

There it is. You have heard such tales before, no doubt. All very impersonal, isn't it? That is one of the "objective", detached arrangements made in the name of family, country, morality, or God. This "impersonal arrangement" was my mother's chief blow in life. It nearly destroyed her. Her parents, when they ascertained the facts, were much nicer to her. They felt guilty for being so cruel to her, apparently. Now that their bleak view of life an human nature was vindicated, they could afford to show a little of their Christian charity.

My mother, bless her, was not taken in by this hypocrisy. She refused to submit to their view or to that shown by the prince's letter. She was determined that she was going to give birth to me and care for me, no matter what. She also refused to let the prince know about her pregnancy–out of pride, naturally. In that, thank goodness, she was fully Greek. If he could not go against his father's conventionality out of love and conviction, then she was not going to force him to do out of duty. She was not going to substitute one duty (his to his father and country) for another (to her

unborn child). She left her farm in Greece and went to Alexandria, in order to be near him in some way. Since she was a talented seamstress, she was able to support herself very quickly.

And so, I was born. It is not, as I have said, a sad, and sordid and beautiful story, all at the same time? Like a fairy tale, is it not? But my life is no fairy tale, as you will see.

I was born at home and easily, despite the apparent curse upon my mother's fate. I gave her no great cause for pain as a child. I was a pretty little thing, with dark eyes and skin like my father, blond hair like my mother. My hair, however, was rather darker and streakier, and not so pure and golden as my mother's. Still, the light hair and dark skin were an unusual combination and I was a point of interest among people.

My childhood was happy. I in no way felt rejected, unloved or cast out, on the one hand, nor "chosen" on the other–as you seem to have felt, Julia. We lived simply, among lots of poor people, but there was enough to eat. The "ghetto" life was warm and cozy for me, and not a horror as it was for you. Julia. You, sir Arab, will probably understand this better. "Quarters" are different from "ghettos", after all.

My mother was not bitter about her fate. She seemed content to be a seamstress, take care of me, and have her small pleasure in life. I played and danced and sang and was petted by everyone–rather spoiled, I think, but not too obnoxiously so. My mother told me the story of my father, which made me feel–how shall

I put it? Not "chosen" or special, but...something unusual. I guess I have no word for it, even though I am Greek. All I can say is that it made me feel good and that there was only one Sybilla. That's it! What I felt was not that I was "chosen" nor "special" but that I was one of a kind. There were no others like me and there never were any others like me, nor would there ever be! This had nothing to do with being good nor bad, virtuous nor talented, just "one of a kind." I still think so, though the many "impersonal" experiences that I have been subjected to have knocked out any special joy in this fact. It just *is* so.

That, my friends, is my background: just a Mediterranean girl born of a Greek mother and an Egyptian father, but brought up on the streets of Alexandria and with father absent. Happy, all the same? Yes. My mother loved me, and all the males around us adored me and bought me sweets and good things. Until I was thirteen. That is another chapter in my short but impassioned life.

At the age of thirteen, my life changed. How can I describe how this change came about? If I use the word "desire", you will, perhaps, understand me, I fear, only in terms of customary categories or values which may be prim, lascivious, natural, ordered, religiously lawful, or some other. These do not encompass what I have experienced as "sexual desire." I can hear some cynic say: "Oh, she just awakened to sexual desire and felt, like all young adolescents, that this was the first time that such a thing ever happened.

I can only tell you it was different, and I think I am qualified to be an authority in this matter, as you will soon see. It happened like this: At first it was nameless–a kind of warmth and good feeling in the body, which combined itself with an itch, a desire to rub and be rubbed. It was a diffuse, but good, feeling. I was reminded of my experiences in my earlier childhood. I had often had sexual play with the little boys of the quarter. We would hide behind the buildings and examine each others' sexual organs–fondling them, licking them, sniffing them, like the little animals that we were. We laughed and enjoyed ourselves a lot, suffering no pang of guilt nor needing more than that. We were healthy little animals, playing.

Which makes me wonder why I was so hard hit when I was thirteen. That is not quite accurate–I know very well why I was so devastated at thirteen, but I did not find that out until a number of years later. At thirteen, suffice it to say, I felt a strengthening of these desires and pleasures, but was, at first, by no means disturbed by it. I understood that sex was somehow more serious–not just play–but I was heartened by it, felt more grown-up, and was not threatened very much. My breasts began to grow and I became more and more flirtatious.

I experimented in love making with several boys I grew up with, but our desire had natural limits and I felt no great shame nor difficulty. There was only one experience which I found disgusting. There was an old man who had been watching me for some time.

I knew that he was lascivious and I was somewhat repelled by his greedy and beady eyes. One day he came close to me and whispered in my ear that he would give me good things if I did what he wanted. I trembled with disgust and irritation and tried to pull away. He grabbed me hard and squeezed my breast. I fought hard and slapped him across the face, even drawing blood with my nails. He let go, and I immediately felt sorry to have hurt him, and even felt some compassion for his need. I said some few words of apology for hurting him and told him that I would have to go home.

That incident reminded me of the time when I was small, perhaps five or six, when another old man gave me some candy and asked me to walk him home. I did so, and he asked me to hold his penis while he urinated. I laughed and felt peculiar–not because of the act, which seemed rather exciting to me, but because he was like one of the fathers, and one did not do that with fathers, I thought.

I tell you of these incidents not because they are interesting, but because they are, in fact, not very exceptional, but could happen to any normal girl. I think that my reaction was normal, as well. Indeed, with my experience of life since that time, I believe that I was healthier than most along the sexual line. If I had been allowed to develop normally, I would probably have had a rich and meaningful love life. My loves, then, might have been pleasurable rather than, as it turned, a story of agony.

No matter. I must try and tell my story as it happened. If I am tempted to justify myself or elicit your sympathy, I will deny the intrinsic reality of my individual experience. I would be horrified to do that. I do not welcome judgments, evaluations, sympathy, or any kind of comment, which is so much "impersonal" nonsense, unless you are ready to share with me what you, yourselves, have experienced along this line! Do I sound defensive and hurt? Yes, I suppose I do. Despite all my efforts, there are still traces of my wounds–they heal only slowly, I suppose.

Enough of my defensiveness. Let me be open about what happened! After this first period of flowering, I felt an increasing intensity of desire. I began to be obsessed with the image of penises, breasts– wanting to suck on them, lick them. At the same time, I was preoccupied with the desire to have my vagina penetrated by increasingly larger penises, which would overwhelm me and fill me up. Nor did I just fantasy about these things! No. I began to find boys my own age and somewhat older to fulfill some of these desires. They were inexperienced like myself and sometimes rough, and sometimes too weak; but even with the older ones, I was never quite satisfied.

I had not yet had orgasm, and, from what I heard, that experience would relieve a person of desire. I began to masturbate and did have orgasm, but found it was only partially relieving. It was, somehow, not enough; I wanted a partner. One day, after a few months in which I was obsessed with sexuality and every day seeking someone out, I had an experience with a mature man. He played with me, licked my sexual parts, had me do the same to him and, finally, had intercourse with me many times. I finally did have orgasm and found relief.

My passion was mitigated only temporarily, however, and I was soon ravenous again. I was beginning to feel guilty about all these acts, without knowing exactly why I felt so guilty. Perhaps it was only a nameless shame. It was not a sexual law that I was violating, I felt, but something in me as a woman. A woman who could not be satisfied with one man, even many men, what kind of woman was that? And love? I did not know what it was, but I knew that whatever it was, my sexuality was not that!

At last, in desperation, I told my mother about what was happening. At first she was shocked, but, good mother that she was, she quickly commiserated with me, and took me to a doctor to see if I could be relieved of this excessive desire and to see if I were ill. The doctor examined me carefully, and I grew quite excited. He did, too, poor man, and we were soon having sex. I both hated him and felt compassion for him, just as I did for the old man before. I realize, and knew even then, that I was as much to blame as he was. I did entice him, after all. I think that I was not to blame with the old man, however.

The doctor warned me not to speak to anyone about what happened, and I agreed. I went back to him again and again, for "treatments". These consisted of sexual activity. This was, I suppose, treatment of a sort, because I had temporary relief, but, of course, I was not "cured." I also could not tell my mother about it, since I did not want to hurt the poor doctor. At last I had the courage to tell the doctor that he was not helping me and hat if he did not stop, I would have to tell my mother. This frightened him greatly, and he promptly told my mother that he was unable to continue seeing me.

My mother then took me to another doctor, and the same thing happened. This time, however, I realized that no one was going to be able to help me, and that I had to do whatever I had to do alone. The second doctor was easily disposed of–he was more a fool than anything else–I told my mother about my real situation. We sat down together and wept. My mother finally told me that since my birth, she had worried that she had violated the Gods. She had an unspoken fear that she was going to be punished for a nameless transgression. She did not believe that she had, in fact, really transgressed the Christian or Muslim God–even though she had broken their law. She had done so out of love, and "dear Jesus" (as she said) would be forgiving. Rather, she feared a nameless God that hovered over her. She wondered if she now, through me, was being punished. She wept, and tried to take it all upon herself, even praying that the nameless God, if offended, should take her and not her poor, innocent daughter. I felt deeply for my mother, but knew that her martyrdom would be of no avail.

I did not know, myself, why this was so–it just was. I had to live my fate as it came to me. When I told my mother this, she crossed herself, and was satisfied. It is Greek to accept one's fate, and it is Muslim also. She loved me for it, and for not blaming her. How could I blame her? Can one blame the storm for thundering and lightning? So, at 13, I became a woman, came to my own fate, and was ready to kill myself. Only my desire kept me alive.

I was a woman, at 13. I had achieved my full height and full physical development. I was quite attractive and had a rounded, pleasing figure. Despite my inner turmoil and doubt, I appeared to others as if supremely happy and full of life. Only my mother and the few boys and men with whom I had relations had any inkling of what was beginning to happen. Mother and I alone knew of its seriousness. We tried to hide it, at first, but it became impossible. My mother gave me cold baths, she rubbed my parts herself, she even gave me her breast to suck on, thinking that perhaps, this would relieve me (one of my lusts was to suck on penises and breasts). I was deeply touched by her attempt to relieve me, but it was fruitless. The lusts would not be denied, cooled or hidden. At last, we both gave up, and I went into the street.

I tried to keep some semblance of decency and humanity, but soon I was known everywhere as the girl who would have sex with anyone. I hated this and was deeply humiliated, but it was true. My mother was laughed at, and soon the decent people (why is it that everyone is "decent" when you have trouble, which is to say that they do not wish to help?) did not bring her sewing any longer. She was laughed at, as the mother of "that nymphomaniac." "Sybilla, the Nymphomaniac," I was called.

Soon, my mother had no money, and we had to earn a few pennies in some way. I strove with all my might to restrain myself for the sake of my mother and I became a prostitute. It was not that I minded being a whore–I was already much lower than that in my own eyes–it was only that I did not think that I could restrain myself sufficiently to charge money for that which I needed so desperately. I would myself pay all that I could, if I had the money.

Being a whore proved to be an effective, though temporary, solution. At last I had a place in life. I earned a few pennies, enough to take care of the minimal needs for survival of my mother and myself. I seemed to be part of the human race again.

As a whore, my experience widened. I no longer had to be furtive in my need to get men; now I could solicit them openly. Since the amount of money did not matter to me, I went with all kinds: young, old, fat, thin, handsome, ugly. I experienced them all. There is little, in the way of sexual depravity, that I do not know. Nor do I put this on the men alone, since I not only accepted, but desire every such depravity. But my desires were never really fulfilled. The horror of it all was that whatever I wished, and would then try to fulfill, would immediately be followed by terrible self-revulsion and guilt (towards what I did not know) and then another desire of equally intense nature. I was doomed to live a life of desire, fulfillment, guilt, reawakening of desire, and to repeat this cycle in such a way as to wrack me with pain and agony. Yes, I know, there are many people who have desire and must go through such torments and conflicts–but I wonder how many of them have had to live them as I have?

Sometimes I would talk to my sister prostitutes. Most of them were frigid–hating men and using this way only to earn a living. They were difficult to awaken sexually, required a great deal, and as whores, both stimulated themselves extensively and earned their bread. Usually, they had a pimp who was also their lover and who, of course, took away all the money that the girls earned. My sister whores had love where they were despised, and gave love where they, in turn, despised. This was the more typical kind of life, though there were also girls who were just poor and found this a good way to earn money. These remained prostitutes only briefly. They soon married or found someone to take care of them. All in all, the girls and women I met as prostitutes were not so different from women in any class of society–they were only more open about things and more independent. The same can be said of the men–I saw a cross section. Being a prostitute, I suppose, is like being a doctor–one finds out about the secret places of men and women: their agonies and loves and desires. One even has the pleasure, sometimes, of fulfilling these, or starting some young lad out right.

You may have noticed that I said "women." Yes, it is true. I had a desire for women as well. Not as strong, but there all the same. And even women would pay me–for many such have this desire also. I laughed at this side of it–luckily I could hardly take that part so seriously. I did mention those who were as maniac as I for such sexuality. I merely nodded to them, and felt that I had to deal with my own madness.

For a few years, I managed to make my way, and had some kind of life as a prostitute. All the same, my desire was not fulfilled, and the epithet, "nymphomaniac", stayed with me. Indeed, I became quite mad with my insatiable desires. After a time, it became known that I would have all kinds of sex without any payment whatsoever, so that no one, now, would help me fulfill my role as prostitute. I was reduced to taking all who came and I had no place in society at all. I walked the streets, clothes torn, almost nude. I began to grow dazed. I think that I finally lot my humanness, and was taken by everyone who wished. I remember vaguely that I was picked up by a pimp who promised me a few pennies.

This pimp had me on stage, having intercourse with animals. I remember it only vaguely, for I was now almost out of contact with reality altogether. The humiliation was total, though I recall feeling that the animals had more warmth and humanity than the people. I remember… I remember…no, I do not really remember. That whole period is more a dream than a memory.

I finally wandered away from the city, out into the desert. I was determined, now, to die. Many times, over the years, I had tried to kill myself, but I had been unable to complete the act. Now, I decided that I would starve myself to death. I knew that I could not control my sexual desire, but had the happy thought that I would soon be too weak to seek out its fulfillment. Hunger, after all, deprived, is stronger than sex! Even when the latter is monstrous!

I wandered into the desert, many, many miles. I walked day and night. I drank (for I found that thirst

cannot be denied! It is stronger than hunger or sex), but I did not eat. I tried to wander far from men, for every time I would see an wandering group, or a caravan, I would still feel compelled to rush up to them and take all of them sexually. At last, even these turned me away, as I must have looked quite terrible.

Then I laughed. Finally, I was relieved –not of the desire, that never left me. I was relieved of any possibility of fulfillment, since I was now so horrible to look at that no one would have me. What had happened to that beautiful, healthy girl who was full of life? At 18, I was near death, and happy to die.

In this state, I wandered; I do not know how long. I came to the Sphinx, and, in a cave nearby, I stumbled in, ready to die. In my delirium, I thought I saw a figure of a man sitting there. With my last remaining conscious thought and breath, I called out to him to take me sexually, and then I fainted.

I do not know when I awakened. Indeed, I cannot, in truth, claim to have "awakened" in any real sense for many months, even years. In retrospect, I see myself as having been totally possessed and largely out of contract with outer reality fro those three years that I spent in that cave. It may be hard to believe, but I spent three years, until I was twenty-one years old, in the cave. One might say that I gradually emerged out of madness, or was healed, or was simply bizarre, but none of these is the way that I see it. I will try to explain what happened, as best as I can.

When I "awakened", as I say, from the initial faint, I was still quite delirious and probably near death. The man who had been sitting near me was now standing and I saw him as clearly as anything could be clear in such a state. What I saw was Christ, crucified upon His Cross. There was sweet Jesus, suffering mightily upon his rack of pain. I cried out, "Oh, sweet Jesus, forgive me!" The figure came down off the cross and gave me water to drink. At that moment, for the first time in many years, I was relieved of the terrible pain of desire and tormented lust that had gripped me every moment. I rested, and knew that I was not going to kill myself.

I wept softly for a long time and then slept. When I awakened again, I was not nearly so dizzy nor vague as I had been with my previous vision of the figure in the cave with me. Now I sensed not him, but a larger-than-life-size figure emerging from inside me. I was shaken and awed to see a huge figure of a male human body, with the head of a hawk. I was astounded by it and looked to see if my companion saw it, too. He seemed not to notice it: He hung limply form the nails punched into His hands and feet, His head falling on his chest. I was full of compassion for His suffering, but was powerless to do anything about it.

The Hawk-Headed God, for such is what He was, I am convinced, spoke. "You are dead and in the land of the dead. What you have heard from your mother is true. On the night that you were conceived, the

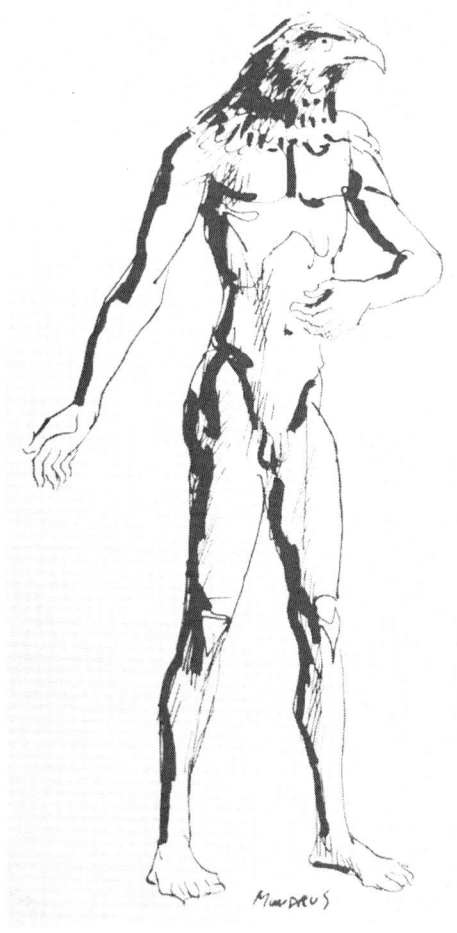

Gods of the Greeks and the Gods of the Egyptians came together. We came together not in animosity nor in wrath nor in rivalry. Indeed, we had not planned to come together at all. It was the act of your parents which brought us together. This is a sin of pride according to the Gods of your mother in Greece, but is no sin according to us, the Gods of Egypt. At first, we merely felt incommoded by the action of your parents, and allowed a relatively mild fate to take its course. But we, like your parents, had not reckoned upon those other Gods, of more recent origin: your Christian and Muslim Gods. We Egyptians have no rivalries nor jealousies–our sway, after all, is the oldest of all. We allow new Gods to thrive. The same can be said for the Greek, but your Christian and Muslim upstarts are far too youthful and rebellious. So we had a war within your soul. (Ha! I find that even I change, for I use the word 'soul' and not Ba and Ka as I did of old. No matter, even the Gods change, I suppose.) In this war, you have followed now one of us and now another. Perhaps now you can understand your desire followed by guilt–different Gods are being served! This conflict has finally brought you to us. You have surrendered, which has erased the sin of pride which your parents had toward the Greek Gods. At that same moment, we came to an agreement. We agreed to have our sovereignty serially and not at one time, for that would kill not only your body, but your soul, too. We do not wish your destruction, but wish you to find peace and even help us to reconcile ourselves with ourselves. We did not ask it, but now we need you. Thus, now, you die to the world and in these three years, you will reconcile us, your Egyptian Gods."

With that long speech, which I remember very well, indeed–delirious as I was–the Hawk-Headed God faded. I was astonished at this and knew not what to make of it. This big impersonal God, with no name that I knew, was now kindly and warmly informing me of the most huge, incongruous thing of which I could imagine. Yet, it made sense to me, and I was strangely stilled once again from the torments that I had suffered. If I was mad, I was glad to be so! I thought of the name I had been given, "Nymphomaniac", and was able to accept at least the last half of the appellation: "Maniac." I laughed: Better to be a Maniac than a Nymphomaniac! The laugh died on my lips, however, for in a moment I felt a huge pressure from within me.

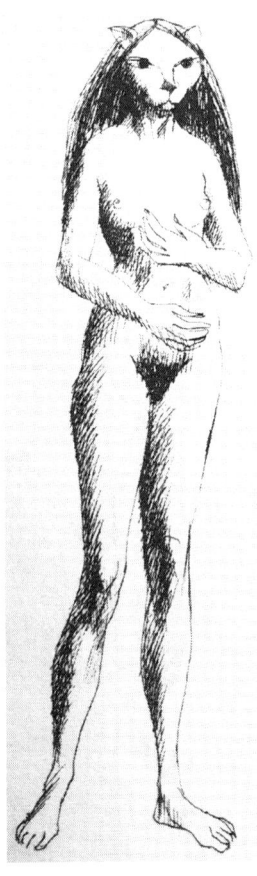

It was as if all the sexual desire that had hounded me and beaten me and tormented me all these years since I was thirteen was suddenly gathering itself into one large unit and forming itself. Then, manifesting first as a vapor, and later becoming solid, there came out of my eyes, nose, ears, mouth, vagina, anus, a figure which gradually grew and formed itself into a creature which was as fantastic and gigantic as the Hawk-Headed God had been. This one, however, had the body of a woman and the head of a cat. This Cat-Headed Goddess said not a word. She merely looked at me and penetrated, with her look, into the marrow of my soul. I was aflame with desire and sexual passion. She then looked from me to the figure on the Cross and I knew what I had to do.

I hope that I do not offend any Christians among you, or the Christian sentiment among any of you who happen to profess another religion, when I tell you what happened. I can only say that my mother, whom I have always dearly loved and treasured, is Christian, and that I am Christian in part, as well. If what I say offends you, perhaps you had best look to your view of Christianity, for I do not believe that it should offend. Christ is God's Son made flesh, is He not? And flesh includes that animal part of ourselves, does it not? And He is a God of Love, is He not? Enough of my questions and apologies. I do not wish to be defensive, for I have, in truth, nothing to be defensive about. So, let me proceed with my story.

What the Cat-Goddess had me do, filled as I was with both enormous lust and enormous love, was to lick this God-Man in all his body. I licked his wounds, and licked and sucked his sexual organs. As I licked and sucked and felt and stroked, I was enraptured in joy and ecstasy. I felt Him come to life; I felt Him as man and as God in His organs and in His Being. My joy and desire and my lust knew no bounds.

The Cat-Goddess drove me onwards, though I needed no prod. The Christ-God responded and came to life. Though I was dead, and in the land of the dead, I awakened a God, and I did this through a Goddess. If all this sounds strange, I can understand that you find it so.

When the God-Man came to life, he came off the cross and left me, saying, "I must be about my Father's business." I wept and wept and again slept. In my dreamless sleep I was at the bottom of all flesh and all soul: I knew what it was to long for soul, for flesh and for connection; for God. Desire alone was as nothing without love and union, and I wept.

When I awakened, I saw what resembled the God-Man but he seemed human to me, not a God. Here was a man, in middle life, whose face was strong, but lined with care. His deep, dark eyes were filled with intensity and compassion. He stroked my head and gave me water to drink. He told me that I had been in a state of delirium, or something very much like it for a very long time–he did not know himself for how long, since, himself, had been in a near mad state. He thought it to be for over two years, in any case.

I was amazed to hear this, since for me, perhaps only two days, and not two years, had gone by. I tried to speak, to tell him of my astonishment and to ask him who he was, but I found that I could not utter a word. He saw my efforts and that they were in vain, and sadly put his hand on my lips, to calm my anxiety. He spoke: "I can see that, dazed as I was, I have been more conscious through all of our experiences than you have been. I think that I know why you cannot speak now. It is my fault, and I will tell you about it later on. Let me tell you, first, what I know, since I can speak and seem to remember and, in your delirium, you told me very much about yourself. I know about your Greek mother and Egyptian father, and I know about your nymphomania and hungers–indeed, I think that I know all about you, though you are not aware that you told me. But you spoke only for a time; for many, many months you have 'spoken' only with your eyes, your lips, your body, your hands. It began when you announced that the 'Cat-Goddess' was now going to act, and that the era of the Hawk-Headed God was coming to an end. It was during the 'Era of the Hawk-Headed God', if I may call it such, that you spoke deliriously of all your past and all suffering. I tended you during this time and nursed you and fed you. That went on for many months. When the 'Era of the Cat-Headed Goddess' came to be, you stopped speaking and then began to touch me and fondle me and lick me and fill me with all manner of sexual delights. I was torn to bits by this–filled with both joy and satisfaction and great guilt and anguish. During all this time, the only words that would pass your lips would be, 'Sweet Jesus.' I knew that you saw me that way, but I felt myself to be anything but a God–Man.

"Which leads me to speak about myself. I am a man, no longer young, who was a well-respected wise man among my people. They called me Rabbi and came to me, as if I were Solomon, full of wisdom. I read from the Great Book, and read it well, because I felt it deeply. It was from this Great Book that I read to you when you were in your 'Era of the Hawk-Headed God'. I am not sure if you understand me, but the sound of my voice, at least, seemed to calm you.

"As I say, I was known as a kind of Solomon among my people, but I felt like a hypocrite. With all my wisdom and knowledge of 'The Book', I was filled with vast and insensate sexual desire is the same as fulfilling it, but I was so horrified by need for every kind of sexual perversity, that I wanted to die. It was not so much the sexuality which horrified me–I am not a prude–but my hypocrisy. I could not preach the Law and experience its opposite in my loins, without feeling the fraud.

In my despair, I prayed to God for deliverance, and was sent a dream. I was told to go to Mitzraim in the west, and there to find a cave. In that cave I would meet a prophetess, a witch like she of Endor, who would show me the way out of my dream within a dream, sayeth the old prophets, is the deeper wisdom of God. In this dream, I saw myself reading from the Good Book. A lovely young girl, looking just like yourself, sat listening to it in joy and appreciation. I went behind a wall and proceeded to masturbate myself in great desire, and great guilt. The girl came and did this for me, saying 'That (the Book) is good, and this (the penis) is good.' She did this so simply and lovingly that I was enchanted. End of dream.

"So, you see how it was that I set out, straight-away, for Mitzraim, and came to this cave. I had not been here for more than a day when you, the answer to my prayer, had arrived. I was immediately overcome with desire, but I had to restrain myself for many months, in order to minister to your needs. And now, for months, you have been ministering to mine, though you did not know it.

"Which brings me to my guilt towards you. You did not know what you were doing. I was wracked with guilt and desire, and continually berating you in my agony. I blamed you, though I was guilty myself. At last, after all this time, I must admit my guilt, and accept it gladly. It was worth all the pleasure, and I accept it."

I looked at this man in wonder and in love. Here he was, berating himself, after having loved and cared for me when I needed it so badly. He had shown me love and compassion and constraint, when no other male had done so. That I could give him what he needed was no sacrifice on my part, it was exactly that which I needed. How could I put into words that I loved him? How could I say anything? He said that it was his fault that I could not speak now. It was not his fault, it was the wish of the great Goddess. The Cat-Headed one, She without love, only passion; She who had hounded me forever without love, would She let me speak?

At that moment, I leaned forward to this Rabbi and whispered, "I love you." The Cat-Headed Goddess had let me speak. Then I and the Rabbi, in full consciousness and choice, made deep and tender and passionate love. As we made love, I had another vision, but this time clearly, and in no mad nor sick vague stupor.

What I saw was this: I saw the Cat-Headed Goddess unite with Christ, the God-Man; She licked and sucked and then He, too, united with Her. And this, while I and the Rabbi were as one.

A great peace overcame us and we slept long and peacefully. But my time with the great Gods of Egypt was not yet finished, nor was my consort.

The next day, I had a vision of a God of the same size as the Hawk-Headed One and the Cat-Headed One. This one had the head of a bull. The 'Era of the Bull-Headed God" began. This Bull-Headed God spoke not a word. He pointed only to the place where my few belongings had lain since I first came to the cave, years before. At His bidding, I fished out a golden coin, the last remnant of my work as a prostitute.

I held the golden coin in my hand and offered it to the God. He did not take it. Instead, He reached up and seemed to remove His Bull Head, which I now saw as a golden mask of a bull. The God's read head was human and bore an amazing similarity to the Christ that I had seen earlier. Was this Egyptian God the same as the Christian one? Dim memories of stories I had heard as a child came back to me. Was this great God called Osiris? Was the Hawk-Headed One his son, Horus? Was the Cat-Headed One Isis? I did not know, for these impersonal, nameless Gods did not leave their calling cards with me, only the flesh and vapors of their being!

In an event, this God gave me the golden mask of the bull and had me melt it down together with my golden coin. This seemed very strange to me. My companion and my love, the Rabbi, did not see the great Bull-Headed God–or if he did, he saw Him very differently from the way I did, but he seemed to know that we had a task to do together. We gathered all the wood that we could find and made an intense heat in a brick oven which we had constructed. From the God's unspoken instructions, the Rabbi and I made a mold of a bull-calf with a globe between its little horns. When the gold was melted, we poured it into this mold, let it cool. Soon we had a marvelous little golden calf with a golden ball between its horns. My Rabbi smiled when he saw it, but his smile changed to a fierceness I had never seen before when I told him that the God required us to bow down and worship before this golden calf. "I will not bow down and worship this golden calf!" he said. I had never seen such fierceness in him and was sore afraid, until I remembered one of the stories he read to me from his Great Book. Then I could laugh and say to him, lovingly, "No, no good Rabbi, my love. You are not to bow down and worship this golden calf, you are to bow down and worship *before* him. That means that you have recognized his power!"

The Rabbi thought for a long time. He did not tell me his thoughts, but I image that the was working out for himself how he felt about gold, about flesh, about sex, about the animal. He said nothing, but he bowed down with me, say to me: "I love you." We knelt for a long time, and then, with a gesture, the God bade us arise. He again had us melt down the gold of our little statue, and this made my Rabbi happy. Jews are nervous, I think, about graven images.

When the gold was fully melted, the God had us do a strange thing–it was strange to me, at least, but not to my Rabbi. The God had us drink the gold. This we did, day by day, slowly, painfully, until we had consumed it all. The Rabbi smiled at this task and was at peace with his God and with the Egyptian Gods as well. He stroked my hair and said, "Oh, my little Mosina, now I know; now I know that you are indeed my witch, my priestess, of the spirit as well as the flesh. Now I have your gods inside me, and my God is not offended. I love thee."

With that speech, which I did not fully understand, he embraced me. I knew only that we were united forever in a bond which was unbreakable. I knew that spirit and flesh were one for me and that I had made him happy. It was enough. At this point, I did not know if my Rabbi were flesh and blood or spirit and he, I know, felt the same about me. I only knew that henceforth he would always be there if I wanted him, and that it was so for him, as well.

We knew, then, that we must part. He went back to his land and his people, and I returned, now twenty-one and truly a woman, to Alexandria.

V

At the age of twenty-one, after three years absence, I returned to the city of my birth, Alexandria. I felt that I had died and been reborn. In many ways it was true. My mother had long since given me up for dead and had deteriorated greatly. She had sought me everywhere, without avail, and longed for death herself. She was barely kept alive by those few friends of hers of the past, but with my homecoming, she, too, was reborn.

I recounted to her (and to no one else, for who else except my mother would believe me?) all my adventures, and she was dumbfounded. She murmured frequently, "miracle" or "wonder" and listened with rapt attention. The story gave her strength, and when she saw me healthy and well, she revived. I had changed markedly, of course, but all to the better. I once again had all the beauty of my childhood, and the bloom of my pubescence, but now I had the rich and full body of an experienced woman who knew herself, found herself beautiful and full of love. My hair had become more golden. Was this the result of drinking the gold, I wondered, or was it a consequence of being in the dark cave for three years? Almost all of my hair had fallen out when I was ill and working as a vessel for the animals, but now it had come back in even more luxuriant abundance. My figure was delicious to behold. Pardon me if I seem conceited. I do not feel self-satisfied. Rather, it was amazing, and a miracle to me.

I soon had many men seeking me out. No longer was even a word spoken about my sordid past as a nymphomaniac, and no questions were asked about where I had been for three years. I said nothing, but held my head high. Very soon, however, my belly began to swell, from the pregnancy sustained in the last month with my beloved Rabbi. I sent him a message via my soul that I was to have his child, and I received an answer that he was overjoyed. During that time, also, I nursed my mother back to health.

Soon, my child was born. He was a handsome lad, with wide open countenance and smiling mien. He was normal in every way, except in one particular: he was born deaf and dumb. At first, I was destroyed by this fact. I racked myself to find my guilt, but found no answer. I then shrieked at the Goddess, the Cat-Headed One, who once again, it seemed, had invaded me and done me damage. I then implored the Hawk-Headed One and the Bull-Headed One who had become human–I implored them to explain this to me and to cure my son if they could. These Gods appeared in a dream and said that they, the Egyptian Gods, were not to blame, that this was a visitation from the Greek Gods and the latter would contact me in due time.

I was placated by this news, though shaken in my happiness. I came down off of my high state and realized how much at the mercy of the Gods I still was. I waited. My son grew, and became more and more handsome. He was intelligent and brave and charming, in his way, but he did not speak. I grew less and less concerned about it, since he did not seem to mind it much and was a happy child.

I lived my own life in an ever more adventurous way. My beauty became known and I had lovers of every kind. Alexandria was a Mediterranean port with Greeks, Syrians, Lebanese, Jews, Italians, French, Spaniards, even Englishmen, and its life was sophisticated and luxurious among the upper classes. The poor–mostly Arabs–lived differently, but they seemed to enjoy the spectacle of this other life, as well. I soon became a part of the aristocratic life and had many rich and famous, as well as wise and powerful, lovers. I was much in demand and, within a few years, had my own salon. My life experience had made me wise to the ways of men, and my years in the cave (though known to none buy my mother) made me wise in the way of the Gods. I was, thus, sought after, and would often think that this must be what my Rabbi had, in his way. I enjoyed this life, and even became a mistress of the King's son. This may shock you a little, for the King's son in reality, was none other than the sone of my father by his wife of the arranged marriage. Yes, it was a sort of incest with my half-brother, but we Egyptians are not so shocked about brother-sister incest as, perhaps Europeans are. Indeed, of old, the royalty was required to have this brother-sister marriage. In deference to modern times, we had a love affair, which was what we wished.

My mother had long since married happily. She had also met and reconciled with my father, who was now King. It was a very sophisticated, exciting life. Only two things disturbed me. I sometimes wanted to be married, but knew that I could not, though I did not know why. The second thing that bothered me was the muteness of my son. Sometimes, when alone, I would commune, in my soul, with my Rabbi, and tell him of my sadnesses, and he would comfort me.

Thus did my life go on until my son was eighteen years old and I was a mature woman of thirty-nine. I was still beautiful and sought after, but I had no one to be father to my son. I was now quite rich, so it was not poverty of which I was afraid. I once again wondered about the Greek Gods, and asked myself questions that I had not raised in many years. I was reminded of what the Egyptian Gods told me in my dream, and wondered why the Greek Gods had not visited me. I became aloof and finally, one night, after the celebration of our birthdays, I had the awaited dream. In this dream, I was instructed, by a body-less voice, to proceed at once to Delphi, the place of my conception.

When I told my mother this, she was sore afraid, but she knew that I was touched by the Gods and that I must go. I bade goodbye to my friends, telling them that I had important business in my mother's birthplace–which I did–and tearfully kissed my son farewell. I told him, in the sign language in which we were both now so proficient, that I hoped that I would bring back good news for him. He assured me that he would be all right, with his friends and grandmother, and that I was to enjoy myself.

Within the week, I was at Delphi. I slept the night on the cold hard ground, near the stone of the Omphallos, as my mother had done, hoping to get a dream or instruction. No dream awoke me and no instruction came. Instead, in the middle of the night

I was awakened by a young man who was trying to make love to me. The boy, about the same age as my son, had huge, dark eyes, black curly hair, and was incredibly handsome. He was fondling me everywhere in a greedy way. His hands went to my breasts and my vagina and his lips to mine as if he were ravenous. I laughed and calmed him. I was suddenly moved to take him to a nearby cave, which I found easily and then gave him all the love and passion that he required. I felt strangely maternal in all this, as well as passionate myself, and wondered what it was that these Greek Gods had in store for me.

We spent the night in love making, but my young lover said not a word. He made many sounds of love and passion, but they were grunts and sighs, no words. I remarked this, but said nothing. The next morning, I asked him about himself, and now I understood. The boy tried to speak, but could not. This is quite accurate–he spoke but it was an agony of stammering and stops and stuttering and explosions which drove him into peaks of fury and frustration and terror. I finally put my hands on his lips to stop him, and he bit me and then wept. He wept long and I comforted him.

When he was almost exhausted with weeping, he slowly and painfully stammered out his story, though now without the fury and frustration. He was born, just as my mother had been, on a small farm near Athens, but was the son of a Turkish father and a Armenian mother. The mother, of course, had been Christian, of the Armenian Church, and the father a Muslim. The parents had loved each other, but not only were their religions opposed, but their countries were mortal enemies as well. The boy had stuttered from his earliest years, and no one knew why. He had gone through such terrible torment because of his handicap that he had many times wanted to kill himself. At last, in exhaustion, he had prayed for deliverance to the God which was beyond nation and tribe religion. That night, he had a dream that instructed him, by voice, to go to Delphi and have a deep union with the priestess he would find there. He did not understand altogether what the voice meant by "deep union", but when he arrived at Delphi and saw this beautiful and exciting woman lying on the ground, he grew full of desire and knew that the "deep union" must mean a sexual union. Which is why he made love to me. If I was not that priestess, please, I was not to be offended, but he was desperate.

Thus was his story. I was touched and amused by this sweet young boy and deeply moved by his suffering eyes, Armenian and Turkish at once. I had not the slightest ideas as to how or why I was to be his priestess. I remembered, with pleasure, how I had once before been a priestess and now I trusted that guidance would come to me. I therefore told the boy all about myself, including my experience with the Rabbi, and I assured him that only my mother knew of this. I told him, too, about my son. After our full stories were related, we lay together and made love–something that we both enjoyed, and something I could give him, priestess or not, to soothe his tortured spirit.

I thought about how I could help him, as he slept afterwards. I thought I saw, above him, an image of a fiery warrior, a dragon slayer, belonging, no doubt, to that fierce Muslim spirit of his. I fancied, too, that I saw that meek and loving Christian-Armenian restrainer, showing pain at every hurt to every being everywhere, and I thought I understood. The spirit of the Christian God, with its forbearance, and the spirit of the Muslim God, with its fiery militancy, were torturing this boy. I had an inspiration. When he awakened, I asked him was he an educated boy, or was he an untutored peasant lad? He told me that he had been to school for only the rudiments of reading and writing and numbers. He knew nothing of the Greek heritage, nor history, and of religion he knew only the superstitions and the basic faith.

My inspiration was correct and I knew what I had to do. I took this boy out to the cave. I took him down into Athens and I made him a home. For many months I taught him myself. First, I read to him from the great Homer, of the Heroes of Greeks: of Achilles, the Dioscuroi, and of Odysseus and the rest. I read to him, too, of Zeus and Poseidon and Hades; of Apollo and Hermes and Ares; of all the

Gods of the Greeks, leaving Dionysos until the end. That fiery and watery passionate God was, I knew, the answer to the youth's conflict between Christian water and Muslim fire. I read to him, too, from the Greek poets and philosophers. And I read of the Goddesses as well, for, thank Heaven, there is no Greek soul without the Goddess. I read and I taught. My charge devoured what I offered. In the teaching, I, myself, learned, for I had not been so well educated myself.

I did not only educate this boy's spirit. We made love and I taught him the secrets of Eros. Thus we lived for three years, and he grew and thrived. With each year, my charge changed. Gradually he began to speak without stammering. By little and little his words became clear. They had force and fire and substance. Soon, he knew as much or more than I did about both Logos and Eros, for I had given him all that I knew. I danced with him, and played music with him. I was his priestess and his teacher and his muse. We were very happy.

In the third year, I had a dream, a voice said: "We are very pleased with our handmaiden. You have done all these things for this boy. You have passed our spirit on to him in body and in mind. You have done this out of love and care. Know, now, that Greek and Christian are united within you, just as Christian and Arab are united within him. You had spirit and flesh, now you have Soul. You are Psyche and Sybilla, the soul who speaks and mediates the Gods. And now you can know what was meant in the word, Nymphomaniac. Nympho is our Greek for bride and you are, in truth, a bride of the Gods. As bride of the Gods, you are also a bride of men. Go, Sybilla, a bride of Gods and men, priestess of the soul, go and find your son healed."

The voice ended and I awakened with a great sense of peace and oneness. My charge looked like a young god. When I told him of my dream, he nodded. He spoke and said, "I have had a dream, too, but now I must be about my father's business." He smiled, and I smiled. We embraced and parted.

When I returned to Alexandria, I found that my son had recovered his speech and hearing, probably at the same moment in which I had my dream. We all were overjoyed, and did not know what to do. It was all too much joy to contain.

In nine months time, I gave birth to a daughter who was perfect well and normal and happy. What then shall I say in words? At forty-four, just before my own menopause, I completed a circle. From my mother to myself to my daughter; a story of women and a story of men–and a story of Gods.

I suppose, ladies and gentlemen, you are wondering why I came here, being so happy and overjoyed with my life. Well, I said a prayer of thanksgiving to

God for all that had happened to me and I wanted to be among those who had also been touched by God. Thereupon, I fell into a deep sleep and was transported here.

I have heard your stories, and know that I am in the right place. I, Sybilla, the Nymphomaniac, a bride of God and men, a priestess of the soul, belong among you. I see there, in the Tree, the sacred Phalli, breasts, and other Parts of the Body, and I see, too, the sacred God-Men. Best of all, I see a changing and revolving Pantheon. What more can I say? I embrace you all.

CHAPTER 2
DEVELOPMENTAL POSSIBILITIES IN ACTIVE IMAGINATION†

Active Imagination, Jung's technique of confrontation with the unconscious, is of central importance to the creation of this book.

Barbara Hannah, in an enlightening and appreciative introduction to the book by Anna Marjula, quotes Jung as follows:

> **(Jung) regarded it (active imagination)– right to the end of his life–as our greatest help and support in establishing and keeping a balance between conscious and unconscious. He often regretted that it was not more widely used by his pupils and even once said to me: 'Active Imagination is the touchstone of whether anyone really wants to become independent through analysis or not.' When I asked him whether I might quote this remark, he replied: 'Not only may you, but I ask you to do so.'**

---

*Barbara Hannah has included this monograph in a larger book on the topic: *Active Imagination: Encounters with the Soul*, **Sigo Press, Santa Monica, CA 1981.**

My personal work with active imagination began shortly after I started analysis at the age of twenty-four, and this constituted a more-or-less regular activity, in analysis and outside of it, for sixteen years. At the end of the year in 1966, I was engaged in a long-term fantasy of being in a cave with a Mother and Daughter, as Wise Old Man, and a child who did not speak when suddenly a Knight appeared and carried off the Mother and Daughter. Surprised, I recognized the Knight as a figure from a dream earlier in the year who said to me that "we no longer had a cause to serve," referring to the Jungian collective as such (I had occasion to resign from my local analytic society earlier in the year). Now, this Knight said, he was trying to get my attention and that he had some tales to tell which might be useful for me and others also. There were several in his realm who wished to tell their stories, too. I was not to be a mere amanuensis, the task requiring my full participation. Would I be willing? I replied that I had a busy practice, teaching, a family and social life, but I could provide two days a week for that purpose if that were enough. The Knight agreed, and then began a series of tales which involved me deeply for a number of years.

The first story of the Knight, a kind of gnostic adventure, was followed by a love story of an Arab, and a tale of a Japanese Ronin, using the Zen Ox-Herding pictures as a base. Thereafter came tales of Julia, the Atheist-Communist, Sybilla the Nymphomaniac, and Maria the Nun. Following them were an alchemical tale of The African, a Kundalini adventure by May the Yogini, the Old Chinese Man who dialogued with the I Ching, and finally a Kabbalistic endeavor to understand the Holocaust by Sophie-Sarah the Medium. A series of psalms by each of them concluded the book. These people each had an individuation story to tell, all meeting at the Tree of Life in paradise. The resultant book, *The Tree: A Jungian Journey–Tales in Psycho-Mythology*, (Falcon Press, 1982, first issued 1975); constituted a new genre, in my view, a kind of science-fiction, in which psychological knowledge is combined in fiction to produce "psycho-mythology." The following book in the series is *The Quest: Further Adventures in the Unconscious*, New Falcon Publications.

Thus, it seems to me, the imaginative method of Jung extends itself into realms of spirit and matter, fully consonant with the experience of the archetypes and is a fitting sequel to his work.

† **The chapter on** *Potentials of Active Imagination,* **was given as a lecture to the Analytical Psychology Club of London at the Royal Society of Medicine on March 15, 1979.**

A revised version was published in *Harvest: Journal for Jungian Studies,* **London, November 1981.**

CHAPTER 3
THE POTENTIALS AND LIMITATIONS OF ACTIVE IMAGINATION†

Five years ago, in the spring of 1979, I spoke to the Analytical Psychology Club of London on the topic of Active Imagination[1]. In that lecture, I surveyed the literature pertaining to Jung's great discovery or invention of the technique of personal confrontation with the unconscious and came to the following conclusions:

A. Active imagination is the outstanding method for coming to terms with the unconscious and in finding one's own wholeness.

B. The method is largely effective in the soul/spirit dimension and with introversion, but is less so in the extraverting aspects of relationship, connection with the world, with body energies, physiology, and with matter.

C. Extensions of the method into "psycho-mythology" and "joint active imagination" were promising, as were related developments in the areas of guided fantasy, magic, and bio-feedback.

---

† A lecture sponsored by Aion Foundation and delivered to the Analytical Psychology Club of London on May 17, 1984.

I wish, now, to review what has happened in the interim and to bring the discussion up to date.

In my previous lecture, I noted that relatively little had been written about active imagination despite the great importance that Jung had attributed to the method. Since that time, several important papers on the topic have emerged, as well as a book which can be considered a definitive classic. I am referring to the work of Barbara Hannah, *Encounters with the Soul: Active Imagination* as Developed by C.G. Jung.[2] This book, about which I will have more to say in a moment, along with a paper by Marie-Louise von Franz, *On Active Imagination*,[3] now constitute, together with the original papers by Jung that I mentioned in the previous lecture, a basic body of information which should satisfy the needs of most people in this area.

While I was preparing this paper, I wondered to what extent the method is actually used, so I polled the Los Angeles Jungian Analysts on the topic. I found that practically all of them (97%) thought the method to be a valuable tool, had used the technique themselves, and had recommended it to patients at certain stages of therapy. Only three percent demurred, saying that they worked more with the analytical interaction, with transference, and rarely recommended active imagination. It should be understood at once that the Los Angeles Society was founded in the Zurich tradition and that several members have even trained or studied there. I would image that a similar poll of London Jungians, particularly Society of

Analytical Psychology members, would produce a very different result. More, I venture to say, would agree with the 3% of Angelenos who focus more on transference and the analytical relationship.

When I asked the Los Angeles Jungians to what extent patients actually made use of the technique, however, I found that only 20% of the analysis found that as many as half of their patients did so. The great majority of analysts (the remaining 80%), found that one-fourth or fewer of their patents did active imagination at all. The reasons given were that relatively few patients were embarked on the classical individuation process, or were afraid of the unconscious, had pathology which mitigated against use, found the method strange. Some of the analysts, however, employed variations of the procedure, such as working with fantasy during the analytical hour, or techniques made familiar by Gestalt therapy or other developments of Jung's technique.

Analysts, therefore, seem to value active imagination for themselves, but find most patients "not up to it" or in other ways not amenable to the process, just as I reported in my paper five years ago. In that lecture, I suggested that active imagination was valuable in the dimension of soul/spirit and not with body or world. I shall return to this issue presently, but first I wish to report on the important work of Hannah and von Franz.

Barbara Hannah's book presents seven different examples of active imagination in a particularly full way, most of them (six) consisting largely of verbal dialogues with only one painting briefly discussed from a psychological point of view. The examples include four modern people facing different crises: one gradually preparing an approach to the unconscious by the telling of stories, another by a struggle with the *anima* and a third in preparation for death. These are all discussed with sensitivity and discrimination by Hannah, pointing out the limitations as well as the successes. Her main points are that active imagination is a search after wholeness, must be carefully pursued as "hard work" and with devotion. In so doing, knowledge of the personal shadow is crucial, as well as the capacity to overcome the resistance of "lousy excuses" and, particularly, the danger of panic. The only danger in active imagination, Hannah reports from her talks with Jung, is that of panic, **since the unconscious is not dangerous in and of itself**. Armed with the integration of the personal shadow, however, one can readily face the darker forces of the unconscious in a natural way, with the proper respect, and not be thrown. This latter point is especially revealed in the long and difficult struggle in the fourth modern example, of a woman's battle with her *animus*, leading to a true union with the unconscious and of the opposites within it.

Miss Hannah also reports on two historical examples of active imagination, which demonstrates that Jung "discovered" this method, rather than inventing it. One case is that of the twelfth century monk, Hugh

St. Victor, who has a conversation with the monk, as I alternately felt sympathetic with him and irritated at how he–it seemed to me–was endlessly trying to improve and perfect this feminine aspect of himself. I was comforted, later on, by Hannah's remarks that his *anima* was herself trying to introduce the problem of wholeness and evil to Hugh St. Victor, but only with partial success. It was too soon, says Hannah, for someone of that age to register and come to terms with the issue. I am glad to say that my own *anima* agreed with Hannah. It is also of considerable interest that we, of the present time, can be aware of the forward-looking trend of St. Victor's *anim*a, while he remained in the dark, Such material provides further evidence for the hypothesis of the **purposive character of the unconscious**.

Hannah's main encomiums, however, are reserved for a most ancient inner dialogue, that of a "World-Weary Man and his Ba"–a 4,000 year-old document previously discussed by the Egpytologist Helmuth Jacobsohn.[4] Hannah particularly values the remarkable discovery by this suicide-contemplating man of the individual nature of his soul, and his capacity to make a tremendous leap beyond the collective beliefs of his culture and time.

This leads us into Hannah's characterization of what it is that we are dealing with when we take up active imagination. Here she recalls a lecture that Jung gave to the students at the Institute in Zurich in May 1958. He spoke, then, of the ancient guidance which exists in us all, that of the "two million year-old man." This "Great Man" in ourselves appears in an infinite variety of images and symbols. He gradually reveals himself in ever fuller and deeper forms as we listen to dreams and test their meanings in life. This inner companion described by von Franz and by Jung, is found in an exceptionally unspoiled form in the Naskapi Indians of Labrador, who exist without rituals or organized religion in small family units. They pay attention to dreams and follow the path that the Great man advises, in dialogue.

I happened to be present at that lecture at the Jung Institute in 1958, since I was a student there at the time, and was privileged to hear Jung. I can attest that it was a very moving experience to hear this "great man" speak about the larger "Great Man" in all of us. It is also instructive when Hannah points out that many of the figures who appear from the unconscious are, indeed, "emissaries" of this Great Man, and only gradually are we shown the depths from which this figure emerges in its state of wholeness. Indeed, the significance of active imagination itself is derived from the "main business" of Jung and those like him who see that the integration of the opposites is the essential task of life. In this, Hannah says, active imagination is a chief help.

The importance of Hannah's book on active imagination is matched only by the paper of Marie-Louise von Franz, "On Active Imagination," delivered at the 7th International Congress of Analytical Psychology in Rome.[3] In my previous lecture, I had available to me only a summary of this important paper, which I quoted. This summary specified four steps in the process: (1) emptying the mind; (2) letting fantasy images appear; (3) giving form to the fantasy figures by writing and dialogue; (4) and finally, ethical confrontation with the material and bringing the results into life. Most other fantasy methods end with steps one and two, and one include the fourth one of ethical confrontation.

Von Franz makes several other important points which I did not report in my paper, since I did not have access to it. One of these, having to do with the body, is especially relevant since one of my criticisms of active imagination was that usually there was not enough body or matter in it. In her paper, von Franz reminds us that the alchemists were doing a kind of active imagination by the mixing and heating of material substances, and the eastern alchemists (Taoists) tried to influence the matter of their own body. Thus, says von Franz, active imagination "is actually concerned with the body, but essentially with its basic chemical components in their symbolic meaning." She also points out that one can do active imagination with inwardly perceived parts of the body, particularly in the case of psychogenic symptoms. She noted too, that in the case of strong affects, Jung used Yoga exercises to calm them, and then extract the image from them with which to relate. I am glad to add this material here, doing greater justice to her paper, and I shall have more to say about further developments in body-imagery work shortly. At this point, however, I want to mention some additional points of hers.

The first point is that von Franz feels that the analyst should interfere in no way whatsoever with the active imagination of the patient, lest the analysand remain passive and infantile. Secondly, she says that magic, the attempt to influence events or the unconscious with desire can have a serious "boomerang effect." We can now discuss what has happened with the "body" issue that I raised during my last lecture.

In 1982 there appeared a book by Arnold Mindell called Dreambody: The Body's Role in Revealing the Self[5] in which the author, an American Jungian Analyst living in Switzerland, presented a way of dealing with body sensations and imagery. His idea of "dreambody" is a re-formulation of the ancient "subtle-body" conception.

In a laudatory introduction, von Franz, who was the teacher of Mindell, describes his work as needed one at this time of great interest in the body, particularly since so many people live in their heads or in intuitive realities. Mindell, impressed with the appearance of physical symptoms arising in the course of therapy, hit upon the idea of letting the body signals, as he called them, speak for themselves. He also saw that many dreams express body problems. Von Franz was struck by the idea that the dream image can be understood as belonging to an "in-between realm, referring equally to the mind and to the physiology of the body."

In this book, Mindell explores the history of the subtle-body idea in various fields, ranging from physics to yoga, from fairy tales to clairvoyance. Here we shall summarize his original contribution in how he works with the "dreambody" in therapy. He begins with a demonstration of how he asks patients to "amplify" the symptoms, by which he means to make them greater or more intense. His six-year old daughter, for example, suffered hiccups and he asked her to make them worse. She did so and imagined herself as a hiccup-maker. This hiccup-maker told her to clean up her room and not watch television so much. She did so, and lo, the hiccups vanished. This procedure of letting the symptom speak and amplifying it is Mindell's basic approach.

One of his methods he calls "working with fingers." This involves noticing unconscious hand and foot movements and asking the patient to let them speak. Here he follows Fritz Perls Gestalt Therapy invention. A finger may say to a patient, for example, "Dig deeper," as it pushed into a palm, thus aiding the patient to plumb further into his own feelings. Another way is to explore "inner pain." One amplifies a given sensation of pain, which is really, as Mindell says, "increasing the strength of physical signals" from the unconscious. A third way is to work the skin and other sensations in a similar manner.

This focusing can lead to movement and dance, including the participation of the therapist. One man, for example, feeling a heavy weight on his shoulders, experienced himself like Atlas. He lunged about in a heavy way which "combined physical exercise and psychological insights."

Mindell also suggest a kind of visionary surgery, in which the patient-dreamer, when surgical fantasies appear, can visualize opening up the body and looking inside to see what is wrong. This can also lead to such things as "vision quests." Mindell gives the example of a man who was a long-distance runner. Dreams indicated that there was more to be learned in running. Dreams indicated that there was more to be learned in running, so the therapist and patient ran together. The latter discovered therein that he could run as a man, but still include the softness of the feminine that was suggested in his dreams. A sort of acupressure is also recommended by Mindell, by which he means the freedom to touch each other to see what the fingers are suggesting. He mentions the case of a woman who suffered from crippling pain in her back. Meditation revealed a fantasy of a pain-maker was angry. Patient and therapist changed roles and Mindell pressed into her back as she did to him. That was very relieving. The pain-maker then said that he was angry at the patient because of her vanity. Her stiffness and rigid posture were in the service of looking young and not letting herself be. When she promised to change her attitude, the pain ceased.

Two final areas discussed by Mindell in connection with his "dream-body" work are that of meditation and dream interpretation. For the latter, he notes that body therapies normally do not include dream interpretation because the therapist may be insufficiently informed about the specific condition of the patient's body or about dream symbols. In terms of meditation, Mindell has some interesting things to say.

In his opinion, meditative methods such as Yoga and Zen, which deal with internal dialogue by suppressing it or by passively tolerating it until it disappears, are likely to be "psychologically impoverishing. Such fantasies return anyhow as soon as ordinary life is resumed." He does note, however, that many physiological signs or symptoms are not to be treated, are not even "problems" at all. They are simply "just so" phenomena, the personality of the individual expressing itself. In that case, the mere apprehension of the image is enough to provide relief, if that is what is asked for. Making body processes conscious, then, is a kind of a *samadh*i, a peaceful opening to a center with a "momentary insight into infinity and timeless existence." I wondered here, if Mindell was familiar with the "Mindfulness" meditation in Buddhism, in which one lies quietly and merely attends to each sensation of the body as it appears, either in silence or aloud. It is just such a meditation which routinely produces the kind of *samadhi* that Mindell suggests.

All of the areas of body-awareness suggested by Mindell are not new in themselves. Body imagery, dance, movement, are all found in various therapies. What is new, I believe is their specific combination in Jungian analysis, on the one hand, and the joint active participation of the analyst is likely to foster dependency or bring about a perhaps hurtful or at least unnecessary intrusion. Since Mindell is obviously fully involved in this kind of joint effort, he seems to be doing just that. Mindell, however, clearly distinguishes what he does, which he also considers to be active imagination, from such methods of directed imagery as that of the Simontons, whose work with cancer is quite famous. Mindell has this to say about their work (5, p. 192, 3);

> **Carl and Stephanie Simonton, in *Belief Systems and Management of the Emotional Aspects of Malignancy*, describe meditative imaginations in which medication for cancer is viewed as a positive force in combat against evil cancer cells. Such guided imaginations are unrelated to the spirit of active imagination in which the "dreamer" himself allows his own fantasy system to reveal what is going on in the body. In my experience with cancer fantasies, the medicines sometimes appear as the evil ones and the cancer as the Self. The attitude that disease is a bad thing which must be eradicated is a conscious concept that needs to be tested in individual cases.**

We thus see Mindell's espousal of the classical analytic position which, like Tertullian, asks the "soul to speak for itself." His active engagement with his patient's fantasies, however, is a departure from that position. In conclusion, I wish to remark that Mindell, like me, has been struck with the influence of the body in analytical work and has developed a useful way to work with it. The linkage with the "subtle body" concept, I believe, is a right one, and a significant departure from other body therapies and techniques which do not, as a rule, include the "soul" in this way.

Another work which combines active imagination with the body in a most individual way emerged some months after my paper was presented in 1979, and done right in my own backyard. As if to answer the question or criticism posed in my paper that there had not been enough "body" in most active imagination, Albert Kreinheder, a Jungian Analyst in Los Angeles, presented a paper entitled *The Healing Power of Illness*.[6] In this paper, Kreinheder describes how he came to grips with a rheumatoid arthritis which was not only causing him great pain but gradually starting to cripple him. Here is a portion of his dialogue which he has kindly permitted me to quote:

> **K: You hold me tight in your grip and do not let me go. If you crave my undivided attention, you have it. Whatever I attend to, I must also attend to you. Even when I write, I feel you in my hand, and always in all parts of my body. I am terribly frightened of you. Why are you here?**
> **PAIN: I am here to get your attention. I make known my presence. I have a power beyond your power. My will surpasses yours. You cannot prevail over me, but I can easily prevail over you.**

> **K:** But why must you show me this power and destroy me with it?
>
> **PAIN:** I show you because I will no longer let you disregard me. You can no longer treat me as if I am not. You will know my power and you will humble yourself before me, for I am he of whom there is no other. I am the first of all things, and all things, and all things spring from me, and without me there is nothing. I crave your attention. I want you to see me and feel me and hear me and to bring me the best of yourself. I want to be with you and closely in your thoughts at all times. That is why I make you think only of me. Now, with my presence in you, you can no longer live the same way and do the same things. You cannot use your mind in the old ways, for now you must give yourself only to contemplation of me. But out of this will come many good things.

Thus began a dialogue in which pain and crippling subsided and insights were achieved. I particularly want to note that the figure who literally gripped Kreinheder wanted attention. This was also my experience of the unconscious. My writing of several books of fiction began when a dream figure of a knight broke into my active imagination and ran off with two ladies. When I asked him why he did that, he responded that he was just trying to get my attention, and wanted to write stories with me. Four years and three thick books later, this knight (and his heirs) was relatively satisfied. Such experiences clearly reveal the intentionality of unconscious figures, who have their own agenda and frequently not at all in agreement with what we have in mind.

Kreinheder's dialogues began to include a totally new relationship to the body, even to experience it as a temple of the goddess. His spirit guide was to tell him:

> **The body is the most important thing. It has been neglected because people do not live within their bodies, but always within their senses and within the outside world, and the body is mostly an object that they talk about and do research upon. But in truth the body is that part of us which is most like God, the place where God is chiefly present. Our senses and our thinking are least of God and the most of man. But in its graceful forms and mysterious functions, the body regains its splendor and its tranquility. If we love the forms and workings of the body and adore it as the God it is, then it will glow with nature's power. It will renew itself and will give back radiantly all the love that comes to it. Even in age, as the body withers, it still is beautiful and God is there.**

This active imagination of Kreinheder took place in his sixties, many years after having become an analyst and having used the method without this body awareness. It resulted in a total change of outlook, and, incidentally, he produced a paper which is at once profound and filled with humor. Let me quote once more from the conclusion of Kreinheder's paper.

> The psychological experience one has when he is afflicted with a disease is that he has been singled out by a powerful invader, that he is totally helpless before a superior power. He feels himself to be stricken and assaulted. But there are always images that enter the soul through the locus of the wound. And if the person will enter imaginatively into these images, he will discover that he is elected or chosen for a larger life than he had before. The sickness that comes is both the executioner and the redeemer.
>
> So now, knowing all these things, I have resolved within myself if the invader comes again to me, I will force myself to look at him. And I will say to him, "You have come into me, you disturbing invader. You have come with your pain, and you have inflicted wounds and disabilities upon me. You have brought me failure and disgrace. But I will meet you. I will see who you are and what you want. Because you have come into my house, I will live with you. And because of your being here, I must live differently. Perhaps one day there will come a symbol, some image of how we can live together. I will expand my horizon to contain you, and you too may find fulfillment in my house.

As we can see, this invader of Kreinheder brought him not only body but poetry, too.

My own dialogues with my body pain, alas, have not been as productive or transforming as those of Kreinheder, but I did have a dream around that time which certainly agreed with what his inner spirit revealed to him. I think it is relevant here.

I dreamed that I was leaving a contemporary city, such as Los Angeles or London, and crossing over a bridge toward a totally different, futuristic sort of city. The bridge itself was notable in that it was of the Renaissance in origin, with very beautiful sculptures at the sides, but was paved in the modern fashion. Approaching me from the opposite direction was a crippled beggar, with only half a body. He had a head, arms and chest, his poor form resting on a kind of wheeled skateboard. As he came towards me, I nodded in greeting, as did he. He then said to me that he was God. I was not startled by this revelation and nodded understanding, whereupon he began to grow the rest of his body, until he was quite whole and vigorous-looking. I invited him for a drink at a kiosk on the bridge, and we toasted each other with wine. Then he held out his hands towards me. From his fingers poured gold and silver coins of every nation and every time. End of dream.

In conversation with this figure, he said that God, indeed was trying to incarnate in every man at this time, and to become embodied and realized in us all. This was essential before we could enter into the new era. Our sufferings of soul and body were partly his, he said, as a consequence of a four-dimensional being entering into a three dimensional existence. He was glad that I recognized him.

I would add my own view that perhaps we–humankind–need to integrate all our religious and cultural values–the gold and silver coins of the dream–before we, as a planet, can enter the city of the future, the civilization of wholeness. The dream suggested to me that the traditional alchemical process of sublimation, of extracting the spirit in matter, needs to be supplemented by the Eastern notion of circulation: matter and body into soul into spirit, into soul and into matter and body.

To return now, to what further has transpired in the realm of active imagination in the past five years, I must mention the straightforward and helpful paper of Janet Dallet, *Active Imagination in Practice*,[7] and particularly the beautifully written lines of James Hillman in his book, *Healing Fiction*.[8] Hillman reminds us, as did von Franz, that active imagination has no other purpose than to "know thyself" and this *via negativa* does not aim at "spiritual discipline, artistic creativity, transcendence of the worldly, mystical vision or union, personal betterment, or magical soul wants and in this way we discover soul. He reminds us that the want of the soul reflects the essential nature of Eros, or relationship, and that the mother of Eros was Penia (poverty, neediness, want). In this acceptance of the soul's own *inferiores*, our neediness, sickness and want, do we truly embrace the healing art.

It is not in Hillman's reminders and beautiful use of language that we find his most significant contribution to active imagination. Rather, it is in his use of Jungian concept of the *anima mundi* that he brings an answer to one of the criticisms of active imagination that I made in my previous paper. I remarked, then, that one of the failings of active imagination was that it did not lead to union with the world, except insofar as synchronicity is concerned. Hillman, independently, has made this criticism of Jungian psychology in general, and has offered an attitude toward imagination which would lead it back into the world.

In his paper on *Anima Mundi*,[9] Hillman makes an articulate plea for the return of the soul to the world. It is no longer the soul of the individual patient in psychotherapy which is diseased, neurotic, and unadapted to the world, but he world itself which is sick. Hillman can "no longer distinguish between neurosis of self and neurosis of world." Subjectivity itself has become dry and split. What is needed how is a reworking of the external, non-subjective view so that the soulessness of the world becomes healed. This is only possible, claims Hillman, by a reactivation of imagination. But, before we consider the cure, listen to the colorful way that Hillman presents his diagnosis. First he quotes his friend and colleague Robert Sardello:

> **The individual presented himself in the therapy room of the nineteenth century, and during the**

> **twentieth the patient suffering breakdown is the world itself...The new symptoms are fragmentation, specialization, expertise, depression, inflation, loss of energy, jargoneze, and violence. Our buildings are anorexic, our business paranoid, our technology manic.**

Hillman adds that the argument of depth psychology that the world cannot change until people change is a defense. "After one hundreds years of the solitude of psychoanalysis," he says, "I am more conscious of what I project outwards than what is projected onto me by the unconsciousness of the world." It is the world that suffers, in its own right, and we "cannot inoculate the individual soul, nor isolate it against the illness of the soul of the world."

Hillman proposes a change from the familiar notion of psychic reality "based on a system of private experiencing subjects and dead public objects, " to the idea of the *anima mundi*, the world soul of primitive experience, of Platonism, of Florentine culture and the mystics. By *anima mundi*, Hillman wants us to imagine" the particular soul-spark, that seminal image, which offers itself through each thing its visible form." The world comes with shapes, colors, sizes, textures: "a display of self-presenting forms." They bear witness to themselves, have their own quality, and what we call "projection" may well be simply "animation." Things come alive and draw our attention. To kill this view by labelling it magical thinking has been the murder by depth psychology of the soul of the world.

How do we arrive at this re-ensoulment of the world, this appreciation of an object's self-display in images? By *Aesthesis*, says Hillman, the aesthetic response in the original Greek sense of perception via the heart. "To sense penetratingly, we must imagine, and to imagine accurately we must sense." In this way, says Hillman, we heal the split between sensing facts on one side and intuitive fantasies on the other, which leaves us" images without bodies and bodies without images."

The heart that Hillman would awaken in an aesthetic response to the world is not romantic, nor moral, nor confessional, nor loving, but is the ancient and Florentine heart which has imagination at its center, rather than cognitive understanding. It is a movement from Saturn and systems and fathers, to Venus, and to psyche. It is a poetic vision, a "calling forth." A cosmology, rather than an ontology or a metaphysics.

What would be the effects of such a change of attitude or viewpoint? First, says Hillman, there would be a slowing down of reactions. "To notice each event would limit our appetite for events, and this very slowing down of consumption would effect inflation, hyper-growth, the manic defenses and expansionism of civilization." There would be a shift from ego and it focus on its own reactions to the quality of the world itself.

A second effect of *notitia*, attentive noticing, would be a shift from the fervor of psychotherapy of saving the soul of the individual patient to saving the soul of the world. This would not be the ways of the

Marxists, but a "therapy of the constructed world's psychic reality."

A third effect would "return value from the subject to the thing where it has been preempted by price." Hillman notices that economics has appropriated into its literalism all sense of values, so that credit, trust, interest and inflation are all reduced to the utterly economic. He suspects that when one truly notices the chair in which one meditates in terrible discomfort and for which one pays $19.95, and contrasts this with the amount one pays for a therapy hour, then the "value" and costs of each might change.

A fourth effect would be that the desperation for intimacy, the "transference clutch, the narrow personalization of love, the fear of loneliness," would be reduced, because a world ensouled widens the narrowing of a psyche dependent only on subjectivity, or on our desires for each other.

A fifth effect, finally, would be the ending of the split between nature and technology. There would be soul in saws as well as the trees cut; "all things whether constructed or natural, by presenting their virtues carry soul."

In short, Hillman calls out for a return to the experience of God in each thing. He concludes that although we all are haunted by fantasies of catastrophe, by the end of the world, what is really happening is an end to the literalist world, the dead objective world of the positivist era. The "pathologized image of the world destroyed is awakening again a recognition of the soul of the world." The *anima mundi* is stirring us to respond to find psyche once more in the world. In doing so, we re-connect with the mystics and poets and we will "value soul before mind, image before feeling, each before all, aesthesis and imagining before logos and conceiving, thing before meaning, noticing before knowing, rhetoric before truth, animal before human, anima before ego, what and who before why." In all this, says Hillman, the re-visioning of psychic reality will let our present paradigm break down and allow a "renaissance of soul in the midst of the world, and with it, from the depths of its breakdown and ours, a renaissance of psychology."

I have quoted Hillman at length because the renaissance of language and imagery of which he speaks is clearly evident in his own style. In earlier papers, one might have felt that there was a love of language to the point where the play with words was more important than content, that substance was sacrificed for style, but not here. Hillman has become not only poetically articulate, but even an impassioned prophet.

This concludes the survey of the work done in active imagination during the five year period under consideration, particularly in response to my criticisms of the limitations of the method. I have omitted a discussion of the further developments in guided imagery and bio-feedback which are now quite voluminous and constitute a separate field.

We have seen that the advances in working with the body and its imagery–as done by Arnold Mindell–departs from the traditional technique, not only by including such imaginative activity within the analytical hour but also entails the participation of the analyst. Mindell, however, is at pains to avoid the path of guided imagery, and wants to stay with the original spirit of active imagination, as described by von Franz.

Hillman, on the other hand, although keeping to the spirit of active imagination also, favours a re-visioning of the whole imaginative process by advocating a re-animation of the world. This is no longer active imagination in the classical sense but requires an openness to imaginative activity which is consonant with the original spirit of internal receptivity. Hillman adds an outer sensitivity to the world-soul which is magical. In my opinion, this does not depart from the kind of spirit that Jung was suggesting in the films of him wherein he speaks of responding to the need of objects for human interaction. Such an attitude seems to develop after a long period of withdrawal of projections from the world, and to come at a time when the *unus mundus*–of which I also spoke five years ago–becomes a central issue. How, indeed, are we going to enliven a world which is free of our projects unless we let it speak to us imaginatively? Whether these two original directions of Mindell and of Hillman bear fruit may be examined once more, perhaps in another five years.

Now I want to look at the possibilities of the extension of the process in the field of "joint active imagination."

When I lectured five years ago, I ventured the hypothesis that "joint active imagination," namely the participation in shared fantasy between two people might be another development in the process discovered by Jung. I gave some examples of just such a process I underwent in a joint drawing series, engaged in by an art therapist and myself, and in a work being done by two friends, Lawrense Kovalenko and Dooley Brown, who were actively writing a fairy tale together. I regret to say that I have nothing further to report on the joint active imagination process in creative work, since no other possibilities have presented themselves. The work of Kovalenko and Brown is now in its eight year, and in their joint efforts have produced considerable transformation in their own lives, but as yet there has not appeared a written work to display it. They do report, however, that the work has gradually gone deeper, well into what they consider the fourth dimension, and that as it has expanded, it has found a resonant and synchronous echo in the works of the most recent physics and physiology. But I must leave that exciting area to their own reporting.

Similarly, I must merely hint a what I have done further in the area of joint active imagination in my analytic work. I suggested in my lecture that the work of active imagination and that of the transference were complementary, that the efforts of the former, according to Jung, helped to resolve the latter and that the capacity to imagine–in Fordham's view–was dependent upon working through childhood conflicts in the transference. My own analytic work over three years have continued along the lines of what I called "mutual process" and I am now even more fully including a kind of "joint active imagination," based on the archetypal foundations of the transference process, in the analytical work. This will be described in a forthcoming book.[10]

Finally, I must report on my own extension of active imagination into a kind of Jungian storytelling, which I called, in my previous paper, "psycho-mythology." My personal active imagination ultimately became a process wherein the archetypal figures themselves did active imagination and had me go along with them! The book I described then, *The Tree: Tales in Psychomythology*[11] (original, 1975), is a series of ten tales told by as many people of different religions, races and backgrounds undergoing their own individuation. It is now available from New Falcon Publications. The second book of the that trilogy, *The Quest*[12] (New Falcon Publications 2021) takes up the individuation process in pairs. The first part of the book is a joint hero's quest of the Son of the Knight and Dog, in which both undergo initiation and transformation, sometimes together, sometimes alone, but in a complementary way. This portrays a process of masculine initiation, but into Eros, as well.

The second part of the book takes up feminine initiation and is a story of Mother and Daughter. The background is that of the Demeter-Persephone myth, and the transformations they undergo include the Greek pattern, as well as the Judaeo-Christian tradition. The final part of the book takes up "threeness" and "fourness" in which the two pairs meet King Arthur, Queen Guinevere, and Sir Lancelot. They all participate in a common search for the Grail and its meaning.

I read here a brief excerpt in which in the Son of the Knight, is undergoing initiation by women. He is now in the hands of the Golden Lady, having already been effected by the Blue and the Red Lady, and learned of love in the flesh, fulfillment and spiritualization. He has spent some time with the Golden Yellow, proving what he has learned, and she now takes him to a house.

> **Inside were great numbers of books lining most of the walls, with swords covering the only walls uncovered by books. Seated near a window, busily poring over thick tomes was a handsome man, obviously a man of both strength and scholarship.**
>
> **"Here," said Golden Yellow, "here is the awful man who was my loved one and lover. But what is he? A warrior and a scholar. There is no love in him." He glared back at her in counter-contempt.**
>
> **A war of words and hatred then began, which I**

was powerless to stop. Or was I? The gist of the conversation was the contempt of the one for the other, that the one was not a man and the other not a woman. Finally, I intervened and said, "This battle must stop. It is of no avail. What, Madame, do you want? Please, Sir, let me mediate this senseless strife."

Golden Yellow pointed to the bookcases and said, "I want to wear the pants!" I held back the scholar and I said, "Then, take them!" Golden Yellow, without another word, reached behind the bookcases and found a pair of trousers. She put them on and grandly walked to the wall with swords and shields. She selected one especially beautiful shield, clasped it to her breast and sank to her knees, saying, "Thus do I claim the rights of the Goddess."

At that moment, it was as if a miracle happened. The cold, bitter, Golden Yellow Lady was transformed into a warm creature, like the geishas of long ago. She wore pants, it is true, but these were the silken ones of a woman, not a man, and the shield was transformed, in her hands, to a great round tray filled with delights.

I was so stunned at the transformation of the Golden Lady that it was some moments before I saw that she was now serving with love and adoration the Scholar-Warrior, who had, himself, been transformed. He no longer wore pants, it is true. Nor was he involved with books or battle. Instead he was dressed in the feminine robes of a monk, and sat in deep inner contemplation. I saw that he was transformed

into a Buddha, actively searching within himself, having abandoned both battle and books. And Golden Yellow was serving him with adoration.

I stood in wonder. Was this the next lesson of love? Yes, I saw it, in both of them: Love in the service of God; love in service and adoration; love in the spirit. Thus did my third lesson in the initiation of Love come to an end. I bowed and silently withdrew.

Notes

1. Spiegelman, J. Marvin. "Active Imagination: Values, Limitations and Potentialities for Further Development," Harvest: Journal for Jungian Studies, 1981, Analytical Psychology Club, London. This paper also appears along with an essay on psycho-mythology and a story illustrating that genre in *The Knight*, New Falcon Publications, Los Angeles, 2021.

2. Hannah, B*arbara. Encounters with the Soul: Active Imagination as Developed by C.G. Jung*, Sigo Press, Santa Monica, Calif., 1981.

3. von Franz, Marie-Louise. "On Active Imagination" in Ian F. Baker, editor, *Methods of Analytical Psychology*, Papers from the Seventh International Congress of Analytical Psychology in Rome, Fellback: Verlad AdolfBonz, 1980, 88-99.

4. Jacobsohn, Helmuth. "*A World-Weary Man and his Ba*" in *Timeless Documents of the Soul*, Northwestern University Press, Evanston, Ill. 1968.

5. Mindell, Arnold, Dreambody: *The Body's Role in Revealing the Self*, Sigo Press, Santa Monica, Ca. 1982.

6. Kreinheder, Albert. "*The Healing Power of Illness*," Los Angeles, 1979.

7. Dallet, Janet. "Active Imagination in Practice," in M. Stein, editor, *Jungian Analysis*, Open Court, La Salle, 1982, pp. 173-192.

8. Hillman, James. *Healing Fiction*, Station Hill Press, Barrytown, New York, 1983.

9. Hillman, James, "Anima Mundi: The Return of the Soul of the World," *Spring*, 1983, pp. 71-92.

10. Spiegelman, J. Marvin. *Psychology as a Mutual Process*, New Falcon Publications, Tempe, AZ, 1996.

11. Spiegelman, J. Marvin. *The Tree: Tales in Psycho-Mythology*, New Falcon Publications, Las Vegas, NV, 1982.

12. Spiegelman, J. Marvin. *The Quest*, New Falcon Publications, Los Angeles, CA, 2021

"Sybilla, the Nymphomaniac" is the second of five stories narrated by women in the ten-tale, *The Tree: Tales in Psycho-mythology*. Each of the five stories–as is the case with those of the men–represents

CHAPTER 4
COMMENTARY ON THE NYMPHOMANIAC

a different religious and lifestyle outlook or orientation, but each is also a tale of individuation, coming to one's own wholeness. A further structure of the five women's tales is that they follow a pattern of the development of the *anima*, the feminine component in men, as described by C.G. Jung. These phases of growth in a man's feminine soul have to do with both what he is attracted to (by projection) and also how the inner feminine changes and progresses in the course of his life, should he pay sufficient attention to it.

The phases of *anima* development for the man begins with the Mother, the first source of life and focus for all of man's initial feminine projections. Mother and *anima* at this stage are undifferentiated from each other. In *The Tree*, this is the background to the story of "Julia, the Atheist-Communist." She herself struggles with the problem and meaning of her motherhood and represents that part of "The Feminine." That she also has a particular individuation struggle in terms of atheism is an additional feature of the story.

The second woman's story in the book is that of the "Nymphomaniac," which represents the prostitute phase of the man's feminine development. In this condition, the feminine becomes more sexual, active, morally uncertain, and is characteristic for the adolescent stage of a man. I shall be discussing this story in more detail later on. To give a general picture of the anima phases–and the stories of women in The Tree, however–I wish to proceed with the other three. The next phase is that of the Nun, where the woman now becomes more spiritualized, sacrifices sexuality for a spiritual reason. This phase is carried in the book by "Maria, the Nun," who, as a Roman Catholic, struggles with her religion and its meaning, as well as the problems of incest. She , unlike "Sybilla, the Nymphomaniac," is more of the modern day, although each of the women is rather timeless, as is the experience of the anima in man, as a rule. The fourth woman is "Maya, the Yogini" who is a Hindu and tries to carry out her own spiritual quest by meditating in Kundalini Yoga fashion. In Jung's sequential terms, she would be the femme inspiratrice, the "inspiring woman," one who can bring out the creativity in the man. And such is the case for Maya in this tale: after much work and suffering, she herself has a salon for creative men and is herself creative.

The final woman's story in The Tree is that of "The Medium, Sophie-Sarah." She, in Jung's schema, would represent the highest form of development, that of "wisdom of God" (Sophia in Greek) and also is the bride of God, in that she is the final mother of all his people (Sarah). So, what was at the beginning is at the end, but in a totally transformed fashion. In this tale, however, the individuation of Sophie-Sarah also includes a Jewish woman's effort at coming to grips with the Holocaust.

So, then, the stories of *The Tree* are meant to be general–that is paradigms or examples of various stages of the feminine and of different religious outlooks–and individual, namely tales of individual people searching after their wholeness. Even though written by a man, I must add, I hope that they also are in accord with real women. Such was also my intention in writing about Buddhist men, African alchemists, etc.: that the stories would be in harmony with the general group in question and with their psychology, yet also be individual. Whether I have succeeded in this effort is for the reader to judge.

But now to further explication of the particular tale of "Sybilla, the Nymphomaniac." Sybilla is a Greek girl whose name already reveals what she is about: that of an oracle or priestess of the Gods. She is conceived at the holiest sit of ancient Greece, the Omphallos or central stone of Delphi, where the ancient oracle spoke out of her depths and gave the wisdom of the Gods. Some said she was mad, some said her messages were inspired, and Sybilla has this same origin. Her appellation of "nymphomaniac," is also appropriate, since nympho means "bride" and the implication is that the person is a bride of the gods, those who bring madness.

Sybilla herself explains some of this in her story, at various points, but the theory that is the basis of her wild state is not given. Her condition of nymphomania, an insatiable sexual appetite, is a consequence of the "sins of the parents." We are told that her simple Greek mother had an affair with an Egyptian prince and this union, frustrated in its marital aim but successful in procreative result, is the source of her difficulty. Her condition is the consequence of the wars of the gods within her. Just as her body combines two antithetical strains of Greek Christian and Egyptian Moslem sources, her soul suffers the combat of even more ancient gods: Greek Polytheism and Egyptian Polytheism, as well.

At first, our happy and beautiful gird has no hint of her disorder, but with puberty, with the blossoming of her sexual instincts, her nymphomania comes into full flowering and she is led irresistibly into a path of prostitution, as the only possible role for a woman whose sexual desire is insatiable. We shall assess the veridicality of this proposition later on, but now we shall only follow the tale as it develops.

Prostitution itself proves an inadequate solution for Sybilla's suffering and she is led into increasingly depraved situations, into zooerasty for example, until she is driven, with madness, deep into the desert. The desert of Sinai is hinted at here, though not expressed.

There in her delirium she imagines that she sees Christ and has sex with him. Later on, she discovers that she has, in fact, been in the cave with a Rabbi who himself was driven into the desert because of his own compulsion sexuality, which made him feel the hypocrite. The two, then, heal each other of their sexual madness, by means of Sybilla's surrendering to the guidance of the gods within her, who both tell of her condition and the way to healing. The two are guided by the Egyptian Gods of Osiris, Horus and Isis, and it is through the surrender to their spirit that healing occurs. We are informed that Sybilla's condition came about because of the inadvertent awakening of these ancient gods through the parental union and it was the war among these gods–Egyptian, Greek, Christian, Moslem–that her madness manifested. Above all, it was Isis, appearing as a Cat-Goddess, who insisted on her animal nature, and sexuality. Their proposal is to allow the gods to speak and be worshipped sequentially, which brings about a solution. In this, there is imagery (the golden calf and its melting and swallowing), which is also healing to the Rabbi.

The healing of the two seems to be a consequence of both the surrender to these impersonal forces and the maintaining of a personal connection between them. Love is both the vehicle and a result of this struggle with powerful tendencies which possess them. Sybilla repeatedly speaks of her pain with the "impersonal" and her insistence upon keeping a personal and individual stance and connection. Yet it is her surrender to impersonality that finally produces her healing and her development from prostitute to priestess and prophetess.

Following the healing which results from the union of Sybilla and her Rabbi, they both return to their homes and live happy, productive lives. Sybilla has a child from this union. He is wonderful but flawed, for he is mute. No answer is given as to why this is so, but the hint is that the process, for Sybilla, is incomplete. Years later, when her son is eighteen years old, Sybilla again is visited by the gods and is enjoined to return to the place of her conception, that self-same Omphallos at Delphi. There she meets and makes love with a tortured young man who himself can hardly speak, not from muteness, but from paralyzingly conflicted intensity. He, it emerges, is also a product of a union of opposites–a Christian Armenian and a Moslem Turk. The healing which emerges is that of Sybilla with the boy who can hardly speak. She teaches him the Greek stories and religion, instructs him in both wisdom and love. As a result, he is healed and learns to speak. Through this healing, the boy unites Greek and Christian within herself. She discovers that she is truly a "bride of God" and a priestess. When she returns home, she finds her son healed as well.

The story, in general, shows a process of initial opposites in the psyche, quarreling and battling and driving the host of this battle, the suffering soul of Sybilla, to near madness. As she follows this process, she is healed by others (the Rabbi and the Egyptian gods) and then herself heals others) the young Armenian-Turk). We are informed, then, that the suffering of the person with disparate background is truly the battle of the gods, and that if we can survive this battle and relate to it, they will be reconciled and we, too, will be healed. This, then, is the theme of "Sybilla, the Nymphomaniac."

Is this theme convincing? In general and in particular? As the author, I naturally believe it to be so, both as a writer and as a professional analyst and psychotherapist. The idea, of course, was initially expressed by Jung in his theory of the archetypal basis of experience and behavior and his work amply demonstrates the wide evidence that this is so. But I have taken this theory a slight step onward and implied that it is not only the archetypal background which may produce psychic conflict, but it may also be the divergences of the parental psyches themselves which caused havoc. I am thus suggesting that there is not only a biological union at the genetic level of two varyingly disparate beings, but there is a psychic union as well, in which the "soul" inheritance is equally joined, assimilated, and conflicted. This view is far from being in accordance with American behaviorism, or the generally extraverted position that the mind is *tabular rasa* at birth and all behavior is a consequence of learning after that. It is, of course, a more nativistic view, an done that seems to be in accord with some facts, but not all. I have seen patients whose condition is totally in accord with the behaviorist position and others whose state is better characterized by the nativist one. I once even had a patient who followed an inner animus figure, as I suggested, and thereby continued on a round of behaviorist therapy with herself! Ah, the paradox: a Jungian therapist showing a woman an introverted way at healing, and as she does so she finds that her guide is a behaviorist extravert! The world, luckily, defies all our prescriptions, nostrums and understandings.

To return to our story: I think that the process revealed therein shows, at least, a tendency of the psyche to heal itself by reconciling the conflicting forces within, and that this healing is both inner and outer, both healing of self and healing of others. Also, it is not just coincidence that therapists are both healed and wounded in the course of their vocation, if they are in it with their whole soul, of course. The image of the "wounded healer" is an ancient one. The idea is that the healer is continually re-wounded by each new patient and that he is continually re-healed in the process. Such is also the theme hinted at in the story of Sybilla.

But what about the particular behavior noted in the story, that nymphomania, a driven sexuality, may be at the basis of prostitution? Is that correct?

My own experience casts great doubt on this proposition as a general truth. Let me detail it briefly. I have only seen three or four prostitutes as patients in my years as a therapist, and they have defied categorization. One had been a prostitute in one period of her life as a way of earning a living and it seemed to have no lasting effect on her. Hers was, perhaps, as Sybilla says, too, in her story, a merely "social" form of prostitution which has more to do with a poor woman needing to make a living when she has few other skills and lives in a hostile world.

Another patient of mind had been a prostitute in connection with her adolescent drug addiction. This is a much more common condition in the present day, I think. The prostitution for her was fairly brief and led to her being more of a high-class call girl and madame. Rather than shame and degradation, however, she had experienced herself as "pretty hot stuff," namely so attractive to men that she could choose with whom she slept. The blow to self-esteem, then, seemed minimal. This woman did have a great sexual passion which needed to be worked through and integrated with the rest of her being, but I do not think that the prostitution itself was the neurosis-making agent. Rather it was the whole social and psychological state of being an addict and in a drug culture. There were, of course, conditions which precipitated such a tendency of life, but I am not convinced they were causal but rather pro-dromal.

A third patient had been a prostitute, was now a teacher, but was a cold and manipulating person. I was unable to adequately handle her importunate desire to have sexual relations with me, so she left in anger after a short time. I think that her case was somewhat like Sybilla, except that she was cold sexually and wanted to have her sexuality redeemed. It was the right thing psychologically, but I was not sufficiently skilled as to bring this about without destructive effect. Some destructiveness happens by "acting out" sexuality, others by not doing so. My work should have been to redeem this through psychic labor–imagination, for example–but I could not achieve this with this woman.

My other general experience with this question comes from a psychological investigation I conducted many years ago. I had just completed the written part of my doctoral exams and had the summer off from my job. A close friend, an anthropologist, and I spent the summer in Mexico, visiting archaeological spots and other tourist attractions. One mutual interest we had was to study primitives and prostitutes, by means of interview and the Rorschach test, with which I had become particularly proficient. Also, our Spanish was pretty good in those days. We, therefore, in addition to studying primitive villages, visited brothels in Mexico City and Guadalajara where I was able to convince many of the prostitutes to undergo the Rorschach examination.

The results of the tests were somewhat startling to me at the time, but have been confirmed by others since then. The bulk of women were essentially frigid sexually and quite hostile to me. Some few were of the "social" type of prostitution, but those who had been at it for any length of time showed the characteristic coldness and hostility. The question then arises, does this condition proceed the practice of prostitution, or is it a consequence of the act itself? It requires no stretch of the imagination to realize that being subjected to endless loveless sex and possible abuse of various kinds can be productive of coldness and hardness. How else can such a person survive? For some, this may be a "chicken and egg" question; the behavior is likely to produce the coldness and hostility and the latter can be prepotent to the behavior.

What does this evidence, supported I believe by other investigations, say about the relation of nymphomania and prostitution? Is it only a projection of the male onto females? Is this just the man's whorish anima and desire that is here involved, bearing little relation to the reality of women? This might be the answer of some feminists and I think they are not wrong, but that there is a deeper understanding to be gained. This might even be provided by the story of Sybilla herself.

The deeper understanding is that frigidity and nymphomania are both disturbances of sexuality and constitute extremes of reaction to that powerful instinct. The disturbance can be manifested either way, depending on how the person needs to react to the stresses of existence. It can also depend–and here is where Sybilla comes in–on the native condition of the psyche so inclined. I saw more than one prostitute in the brothels of Mexico who was both frigid and nymphomaniac. This was the type who could not be easily aroused, but longed for arousal and was troubled by the routinely "quick" performance of the male customers. There was much folklore and jocularity in one brothel about men who were particularly able to maintain long sexual activity and such men were much sought-after. And all this to say nothing of the occasional relation with the pimps, (for those not in brothels, but were street-walkers or were in "private practice"), who provided what there was of love.

All this is to say that the story of Sybilla is psychologically true for some people, men and women, who are faced with a sexuality gone amok and require healing. In any event, even if it does not conform to social or clinical explanations of sexual disturbance, there is an imaginal truth to such tales, this also because they conform with myths, the stories of the soul, which take us deeper into psychic truth and, by being general, can comfort the soul. So do I hope with this tale. Should it offend; like Sybilla, I beg pardon. We are all Sybillas somewhere, we are all possessed, sell ourselves, need redemption, and we all, therefore, can participate in her story. I seek a deeper truth and redemption, and not to categorize nor to explain. As a writer, I also seek to entertain, and I trust this, too, will find a companionable audience.

Some Other Titles From New Falcon Publications

Aha! The Sevenfold Mystery of the Ineffable Love –Aleister Crowley
Bio-Etheric Healing –Trudy Lanitis
Undoing Yourself With Energized Meditation and Other Devices
Secrets of Western Tantra: The Sexuality of the Middle Path
Dogma Daze –Christopher S. Hyatt, Ph.D.
Rebels & Devils; The Psychology of Liberation
–Edited by Christopher S. Hyatt, Ph.D.
Aleister Crowley's Illustrated Goetia
Sex Magic, Tantra & Tarot: The Way of the Secret Lover
Taboo: Sex, Religion & Magick –C. Hyatt, Ph.D., and DuQuette
Pacts With The Devil
Urban Voodoo: A Beginner's Guide to Afro-Caribbean Magic
–Jason Black and Christopher S. Hyatt, Ph.D.
The Psychopath's Bible –Christopher S. Hyatt, Ph.D., and Jack Willis
Ask Baba Lon –Lon Milo DuQuette
Aleister Crowley and the Treasure House of Images
–J.F.C. Fuller, Aleister Crowley, Lon Milo DuQuette and Nancy Wasserman
Enochian Sex Magic and How To Workbook
–Aleister Crowley, Lon Milo DuQuette and Christopher S. Hyatt, Ph.D.
Enochian World of Aleister Crowley –DuQuette and Aleister Crowley
Info-Psychology
Neuropolitique
The Game of Life
What Does WoMan Want? –Timothy Leary, Ph.D.
Rebellion, Revolution and Religiousness –Osho
Reichian Therapy: A Practical Guide for Home Use –Dr. Jack Willis
Woman's Orgasm: A Guide to Sexual Satisfaction
–Benjamin Graber, M.D., and Georgia Kline-Graber, R.N.
Shaping Formless Fire
Seizing Power
Taking Power –Stephen Mace
The Illuminati Conspiracy: The Sapiens System –Donald Holmes, M.D.
An Insider's Guide to Robert Anton Wilson –Eric Wagner
The Secret Inner Order Rituals of the Golden Dawn –Pat Zalewski
Nonlocal Nature: The Eight Circuits of Consciousness
–James A. Heffernan
on What is –Ja Wallin

Other Titles by Dr. Israel Regardie

A Garden of Pomegranates
A Practical Guide to Geomantic Divination - A Small Gem
Attract and Use Healing Energy - A Small Gem
Be Yourself - A Guide to Relaxation and Health
Ceremonial Magic
Dr. Israel Regardie's Definitive Work on Aleister Crowley,
  The Eye In The Triangle
Healing Energy, Prayer and Relaxation
How To Make and Use Talismans - A Small Gem
My Rosicrucian Adventure
Mysticism, Psychology and Oedipus - A Small Gem
Teachers of Fulfillment
The Art and Meaning of Magic - A Small Gem
The Body-Mind Connection, A Path to Well-Being - A Small Gem
The Complete Golden Dawn System of Magic
The Complete Golden Dawn System of Magic Book 1 - Ltd. Edition
The Complete Golden Dawn System of Magic Book 2 - Ltd. Edition
The Complete Golden Dawn System of Magic - The Black Edition
The Eye in the Triangle: An Interpretation of Aleister Crowley
The Golden Dawn Audio CDs, Vol. 1, Vol. 2, and Vol. 3
The Legend of Aleister Crowley
The Magic of Israel Regardie
The Middle Pillar
The Philosopher's Stone
The Portable Complete Golden Dawn System of Magic
The Tree of Life
The Wisdom of Israel Regardie - Vol. I
  Selected Introductions, Prefaces and Forewords
The Wisdom of Israel Regardie - Vol. II
  Selected Essays and Commentaries
The Wisdom of Israel Regardie - Vol. III
  Selected Articles, Introductions, Prefaces and Forewords
What You Should Know About the Golden Dawn
Aha! (Dr. Israel Regardie and Aleister Crowley)
Roll Away The Stone/The Herb Dangerous
  (Dr. Israel Regardie and Aleister Crowley)

MANY OF OUR TITLES AVAILABLE ON KINDLE!
Please visit our website at http://www.newfalcon.com

NEW FALCON PUBLICATIONS

*Publisher of Controversial Books and CDs
Invites you to visit our website*

www.newfalcon.com

- Browse the online catalog of all our great titles, including books by Israel Regardie, Christopher S. Hyatt, Robert Anton Wilson, Aleister Crowley, Timothy Leary, Osho, Lon Milo DuQuette and many more.
- Get special discounts
- Order our titles through our secure online server
- Find products not available anywhere else
    – One of a kind and limited availability products
    – Special packages
    – Special pricing
- And much, more more